DAD, MOM
AND THE
CHURCH

Charles Paul Conn

DAD, MOM

Raising Children Together

AND THE

CHURCH

Pathway
P·R·E·S·S
CLEVELAND, TENNESSEE 37311

■

ISBN: 0-87148-267-3

Library of Congress Catalog Card Number:

89-062865

Copyright © 1989

PATHWAY PRESS

Cleveland, Tennessee

Printed in the United States of America

DEDICATION

TO DR. AND MRS. M.G. McLUHAN

*the "Dad and Mom" whose loving
parental style produced a daughter
who became my wife*

Dad, Mom and the Church: Raising Children Together by Charles Paul Conn has been designated in the Church Training Course program as CTC 708. The certificate of credit will be awarded on the basis of the following requirements:

1. The written review and instructions for preparing the review are listed on page 144. The written review must be completed and evaluated by the pastor or someone he designates. Then the name of the student must be sent to the state office. (No grade will be given for the written review.)

2. The book must be read through.

3. Training sessions must be attended unless permission for absence is granted by the instructor.

4. The written review is not an examination. It is an overview of the text and is designed to reinforce the study. Students should search the text for the proper answers.

5. If no classes are conducted in this course of study, Church Training Course credit may be secured by home study.

A training record should be kept in the local church for each person who studies this and other courses in the Church Training Course program. A record form (CTC 33) will be furnished upon request from the state office.

CONTENTS

■

PREFACE

∎

Even for such a small book as this one, there are many people to thank.

Much of the impetus for this project came from the staff of the International Department of Youth and Christian Education; I appreciate their urging me to prepare this volume and their concern for the issue which I discuss in it. I am especially grateful to David Sustar, who was my liaison from the department, for his patience and gentlemanliness during the process.

For someone who is both writer and teacher, the things he writes and the things he teaches are hopelessly intertwined, and many of the things I write within these pages I have taught before various audiences in a wide diversity of settings. I am grateful for all those who have listened, and read, and questioned, and in so doing have helped to shape my own philosophy of discipleship.

Obviously, this book draws on a great deal of material which has appeared in other forms throughout the last few years of my ministry. Particularly I must acknowledge the overlap with several other works which I have published elsewhere. Much of the material in chapters 12 and 13 appeared previously in the book *FatherCare,* and I appreciate my friends at Word Books for their cooperation. The concepts explored in chapters 11 and 14 are also treated in similar form in two books which I coauthored with Dr. Bill Mitchell: *The Power of Positive Students* and *The Power of Positive Parents.*

I also wish to express appreciation to Floyd Carey, Hoyt Stone and my other good friends at Pathway Press for their help in bringing it all together.

Finally, let me mention a matter of semantic style. When writing about parents, youth workers and teenagers, one would obviously wish to write in a completely gender-free manner. Obviously, most of what is said in this book is intended to refer to both males and females unless otherwise stated. Unfortunately, the English language does not yet include a set of gender-free pronouns; all the combinations of "he or she" which are commonly used are awkward and, over the length of a book, become tedious to the reader.

So, until someone works out a better way to do it, I will continue to use masculine pronouns in their classic generic sense. I hope I may be allowed this indulgence without being judged as unaware of female sensitivities in this area.

The best youth workers, like the best parents, might be either he or she, as the text of this book certainly conveys.

1

A
FELLOW STRUGGLER

■

This is the book I have always been reluctant to write.

Over the last dozen years, the idea has been suggested to me several times by several different publishers: "Why not write a book about bringing up children in the church?" I have always responded with an immediate and nonnegotiable "No" for the very simple reason that I am myself a parent of growing children.

The reason such an idea has so often been proposed is that by training I am a psychologist, in particular a developmental psychologist, who studies the process of growth and development in children and adolescents. To go along with that background, I have certainly spent a lifetime in the church, and I am a writer, so the idea of writing about this subject seems a logical one.

But the reasons for my reluctance are quite logical too: (1) I have three teenagers of my own, and (2) I am not sure a psychologist knows any more about the subject than anyone else. When the first definitive book is written that answers all the questions of Christian parents on this subject, I will be gratefully *reading* it, not writing it.

I am not an expert on spiritual development in children and adolescents, and I do not think such an expert truly exists. When I agreed to write this book, it was as a "fellow struggler," to borrow a phrase— as a parent and church member who has worked, and is working still, to accomplish the task this book explores.

This book discusses the partnership between the home and the congregation in bringing its young people fully into the family of God. My best qualification for writing it is the fact that I am a member of both a home and a congregation which take that process very seriously and are currently engaged, however imperfectly, in the process. As a parent I am the father of two daughters, ages 20 and 18, and a 15-year-old son. As a church member I am part of the Westmore Church of God, whose ministers and families have made the discipling of young people a major priority.

So the perspective I bring is primarily that of a parent and a church member. In addition, there are a few other elements of personal background which color what I say here and which have produced the observations that emerge: my work as a minister of youth in a local church and my work as a part of the staff of a Christian college.

For four years in the late 1960s, I served as minister of youth at the Mount Paran Church of God in Atlanta, Georgia. Those years profoundly affected everything that has followed in my ministry. They were years of intense involvement with teenagers, up close and personal, with the powerful mixture of pleasure and heartbreak that every local youth pastor will recognize. There is in that ministry a sense of immediacy and personal urgency that is very rare. It is almost like experiencing adolescence a second time, complete with all its emotional turmoil and richness, with the difference that the youth minister has an adult understanding of the powerful implications of it all; he knows how high the stakes are and how deadly serious the game of adolescence is.

A second part of life which influences this book is my ministry in a Christian college. Dr. Lamar Vest, when he came to Lee College as president in 1984, was fond of saying that he regarded the assignment as merely an extension of his ministry in youth work. I understand exactly what he meant. There are 1,500 students at Lee College, most of them still very young men and women who have not yet completed the process of becoming disciples. Lee College ministers to them in ways which are often similar to that of a local church; and as president of the college I feel more like a pastor than an executive most of the time.

Just a few months before hundreds of Pentecostal freshmen flood our campus each fall, they are teenagers in congregations all across the country, still very much a part of the two families which have given them birth—the natural family and the church family. Today they are your children; soon they become our students. In that sense, I have never stopped being a "minister of youth." During the 18 years I have been at Lee College, I have struggled almost daily with the spiritual and emotional results of what has happened in those homes and churches. Usually the results are very good; sometimes they are not. In either case, we are all partners together in the continuing saga of someone's life.

This book must be written because the need is greater than ever before for a partnership between parents and parishioners who are committed to the discipling of their children. If you thought the '60s, '70s and '80s were periods of stress and alienation in American homes and congregations, fasten your seat belt: the '90s will make the past seem pale by comparison.

Is it more difficult for people growing up today to develop a mature walk with God than it was for us in earlier generations?

That question has been around since "generations" were invented. (Adam and Eve might well

14

have discussed whether serving God was tougher for Cain and Abel than for them.) Are these days *really* worse than the good ol' days, or is it just our imagination?

The fashionable answer to that age-old question is that things are about the same from one generation to the next, that expressing too much alarm about the evil of this generation, as compared with any other, is a pastime for little old ladies with buns on their heads who play "Ain't It Awful!" from their pews at the front of the church.

After all, the reasoning goes, how could the problems of growing up for God get any worse? Is sin any more sinful than it ever was? Hasn't there been a record of murder and lust and treachery throughout the history of man? Couldn't it be true that things are about the same as always, but we just know more about what is going on than we did before? Is it really possible for evil to be greater in one generation than in another?

Unfortunately, the answer is yes! Evil can be greater in one time than in another, and there is a great deal of evidence that the generation in which our children live today is more powerfully dominated by evil than any other generation in history. That is not just an attitude of a few alarmists and sensationalizers; it is true. It *is* harder to bring up a young man or woman to love and serve Christ than it has ever been before.

The reason the 1990s will be worse than earlier generations is not that the evil of any individual is worse but that its power to spread and corrupt others is so much greater.

2

AN UNPRECEDENTED POWER OF EVIL

■

A few years ago my wife, Darlia, and I were driving down the highway with my son, Brian, and two of his friends in the backseat. Brian was then 8 years old, as were his friends, both of whom were sons of families from our local Church of God congregation.

Darlia and I were engrossed in our own conversation and were barely aware of the childish noise in the backseat. The boys were apparently having a good time talking about whatever 8-year-olds talk about, which I would have guessed to be skateboards and cartoons and such. Occasionally there would be bursts of laughter as the boys traded jokes and funny stories.

At some point, as our adult conversation lulled, I found myself idly eavesdropping on the boys' fun. To my utter shock, I realized my son, Brian, was telling a joke about cocaine. And as he finished, there were gales of laughter from his friends, indicating that they understood exactly what he was talking about. Then they took turns with their own jokes, chattering away in squeaky, high-pitched little-boy voices, regaling one another with funny stories, all of which shared the theme of use and abuse of various illegal drugs.

I was horrified. This was my sweet, round-faced little boy, and these were his church friends from the "best" families in town. They were barely off their tricycles, still years away from shaving and learning to drive, obviously not even near their time of adolescent rebellion. Yet here they were prattling away, not about Popeye or earthworms but about cocaine! And with enough shared knowledge on the subject that their jokes made sense to one another!

These were not street kids; they were from old-fashioned, overprotected, sheltered homes like yours and mine. As I drove and listened, I could only think, *Where do they get this stuff? Where do they learn all these things?* What made it so sinister was that it seemed so natural, so commonplace. They were not talking as if they had something to hide, as if they feared being overheard by the parents in the front seat. *It was just a cocaine joke, Dad; no big deal.*

It was obvious to me that this was a natural part of their culture, of their society. Life for my little boy will be lived in a world that includes cocaine. Period. There is nothing I can do about that. And not just cocaine but promiscuous sex, and lying and cheating in business and on Wall Street, and filthy language as normal conversation style, and abortion on demand, and the unchallenged presumptions of atheistic humanism, and public contempt for ministers and organized religion, and much more. Those characteristics will form the dominant motif of the culture in which my children will live.

It is often argued that society has always been evil, that things are not much different today than in earlier times. That is partially true. The evil of the world does not change very much from one generation to the next. But what *does* change is the power of that evil society to invade and penetrate Christian homes. Such a change has occurred with dramatic speed during the past generation.

My son's backseat conversation illustrated to me the power of the evil culture to reach into my home and affect my child. He and his buddies did not learn about cocaine from me or his sisters nor from their Sunday school teacher; they didn't pick up this small germ of modern society at home—but neither was the vigilance of strong Christian homes capable of stopping it, of screening it out and preventing their exposure to it.

The day of the airtight, sinproof, hermetically sealed Christian home is past. Overprotective parenting does not work anymore. A watchful father cannot be vigilant enough, however hard he works at it, to prevent the exposure of his child at an early age to the mind-set and moral diseases of an evil society. A man's home is his castle? Not anymore.

That is what has changed in our generation. The evil of individual men and women is no greater than it ever was, but the power of that evil to affect our kids is far greater than ever before. Sin is still just sin—no more, no less. But the technology of the 1990s gives the sin of individual men and women the power to snare and damn millions of others to a degree that was not imagined in the days of famous sinners of the past like Judas or Caligula or Al Capone.

It would be difficult to outdo any of these men in one's level of personal evil. One can hardly become more sinful than a man like Nero, who dipped Roman Christians in hot tar and burned them as torches to light his garden parties. But heinous as that was, it affected only a very few Christians. The actual impact on the moral environment of any particular Christian home of that day might well have been minimal. The conditions along Prostitute's Row in the days of Victorian London was perhaps as dreadful as anything we have in the 1980s, but a Christian mother in a village 100 miles away could certainly prevent that evil from having any impact at all on her school-age youngsters.

The depth of evil in an individual heart does not get worse from one generation to the next. The development of new technologies has sharply increased the power of that evil to spread and has reduced correspondingly our ability as parents to create safe environments for our children.

Nero, with his evil, could slaughter only a few thousand victims by use of sword and spear. With the new technology called gunpowder, the equally evil Napoleon could kill tens of thousands. By the time Hitler came along, the technologies of the airplane and the gas chamber increased his destructive range into the millions. Now we have the even more advanced technologies of nuclear weapons and satellite warfare, so that the next great madman can butcher more victims with the touch of a button than could Hitler with all his bombers and cattle cars.

The most obvious of the great evils we face today have been present in every generation. Sexual license, drug abuse, violence and a nontheistic worldview appear in the history of every society. But never has there been a period like this generation, in which there is a technology capable of putting those forces at work inside the Christian family.

The "global village" of which sociologist Marshall McLuhan wrote has arrived. The attitudes which emerge in one nation are transmitted almost immediately to every other. A moral atmosphere gains power as it spreads. The underlying values of a fiercely secular society reach our children in a thousand subtle ways: in the cartoons a child watches on television, in the advertising in magazines and bill-boards, in the training of teachers in state universi-ties, in the media images and the popular music, in the clothing and cereal boxes.

Is it possible to isolate children from this culture, to keep it from reaching them until they are older and can respond to it as mature adults? No. Not unless you can keep them from driving down the highway, walking through a shopping mall, inter-acting with other children or otherwise pursuing a normal 1990s life. It is no more possible to isolate kids from the evil in modern society than it is to isolate a growing fish from water.

Not only is modern society better able to communicate its secular message to our children, but the complexity of contemporary life makes it far tougher for a conscientious parent to know how to separate the child's world into categories of good and bad.

An example: At one time most Christians refused to support any business which traded in sinful commodities, such as alcohol or tobacco. Christian parents taught their children not to eat in restaurants that served liquor and certainly not to buy a maga-zine from a company that sold soft-core pornogra-phy. As a child I was taught: "We don't do business with people whose hands are dirty. We don't sup-port the devil's work." We traded with fellow Christians whenever possible, or at least refused to put our dollars into the hands of people who sold liquor or smut.

This stance was an important part of the value system of most conservative Christian families. It also was an effective way of teaching the principle of biblical separation. By refusing to deal with those who made their profits from sin, we taught our children that Christians are not only to live in a personally sin-free manner but are to make a statement by the businesses they support and the manner in which they spend their money. "We don't smoke, we don't chew, and beyond that . . . we don't go with boys who do!"

But times have changed.

The complexity of the contemporary business world makes this powerful form of teaching unavailable for today's parent. It is virtually impossible to separate the white hats from the black hats. How does a family choose to support the good and boycott the bad when good and bad are hopelessly intermingled in the marketplace?

The supermarket where Mom buys her groceries is likely to have beer and wine on the aisle between the frozen foods and the toilet paper. When the kids get on an airplane to visit Grandma, friendly, wholesome-looking flight attendants sell whiskey to the people seated next to them.

So you want to boycott loathesome purveyors of

sin? That is difficult to do when the leading Evangelical book publishers are owned by the same conglomerates that produce R-rated movies. It takes some of the moral satisfaction out of boycotting a movie like *The Last Temptation of Christ* when one learns that the people who produced it work for the same corporate giant that produced the Bible commentary he is using to teach Sunday school.

Refusing to shop in a particular supermarket because wine is sold there seems less important after one learns that Taylor Wine Company itself is owned by Coca-Cola!

The point is that society is becoming increasingly complex, making simple answers and strategies of isolation less viable as a means of producing godly children. This is not to say that the biblical mandate of living separated lives is any less binding but that such separation can rarely be achieved or taught by literal cultural *isolation* from the evil in this world. It must instead be developed by an internal and spiritual *insulation* which enables growing children to be in this world but not of it.

There are two safe havens for the child in this sinful society: one is the home; the other is the church. The child has a natural family of Dad and Mom and a spiritual family of the local congregation. In the context of each family, a growing child can find support, encouragement and the truth about God which will insulate him from the poison of an evil world. Each of these two families—home and church—are best understood not as walled monasteries but as military forts.

In a monastery the Christian remains forever, always detached and sheltered from the larger world, avoiding its dangers by refusing to confront it. A fort, on the other hand, is a place where we train our children to fight and defend themselves, give them spiritual weapons with which to wage war against the enemy, and offer a place to retreat between battles.

Church and home must be partners in this process, because the day in which we live demands it.

CHAPTER
CHAPTER

3

PROMISE
WITH A PREMISE

■

One verse from the Old Testament serves as a
working motto for churches and parents who are
partners in developing disciples: "Teach a child to
choose the right path, and when he is older he will
remain upon it" (Proverbs 22:6, *TLB*).

This verse is both a prescription and a promise.

It is most commonly offered as a promise, reas-
suring parents that all their prayers and efforts will
ultimately bear fruit in the lives of their children.
Like all biblical promises, it can be counted on to be
absolutely reliable; it is from God's Word, so it will
remain true 100 percent of the time.

But it is also a prescription. In addition to offering
a promise, it prescribes a certain type of action;
therefore, the reassurance it offers depends on that
action's having been taken. In every one of these

"prescriptive promises" found in the Bible, we can insert the words "If we . . . " in front of the promise. The "if" clause is a statement of the behavior which must occur before the promise is effective. When we do not meet the conditions of the "if," the promise that completes the verse is null and void.

In reading Proverbs 22:6, have you ever wondered about the number of cases which seem to be exceptions to this promise? How often, when you hear of a wayward son or daughter who has left the faith of his family and local congregation, never to return, have you wondered whether this biblical promise has somehow failed?

This apparent "failure" of a biblical promise becomes understandable when the verse is viewed as the prescriptive statement of a basic principle: "*If we* teach a child to choose the right path, *then* when he is older he will remain on it." When we understand the verse this way, the emphasis falls very heavily on *our* behavior, rather than on God's provision alone. The verse tells us that our good seed will bear good fruit, but first it must be sown; our teaching will not be ineffective, but still the teaching must be done.

So this most-favorite Bible promise of parents and youth workers depends on whether or not we have done our part properly to begin with. Our part is clear: "Teach a child to choose the right path."

This is one of those cases in which it is helpful to

consult a second translation along with the King James Version. The traditional rendering in the King James is very familiar: "Train up a child in the way he should go: and when he is old, he will not depart from it." Though the wording in *The Living Bible* is not very different, the slight difference helps to illuminate the critical emphasis of the entire verse. The most basic emphasis—and that on which the prescription depends—is that the child must learn to *choose* the right path.

The critical task in bringing up children for God is teaching them to choose. Our essential task is not forcing them to obey, not keeping them sheltered from life's complexity, not extracting from them a passive acceptance of our particular orthodoxy, but teaching them to choose for themselves the things of God. All our efforts as parents and youth workers must work toward that result. Then, when we have taught them to "choose the right path," we can depend on the promise which completes the verse. We can be assured that when they are older they will "remain upon it."

An old Chinese proverb says it this way: "If you give a child a fish, he eats for a day; if you teach him how to fish for himself, he eats for a lifetime." Our job is not just to give fish to our children but to teach them to fish for themselves.

A discipling strategy which follows this prescription can be difficult for us to accept. Such an approach has several implications:

1.   We must allow our children to become aware of the various alternatives to our particular philosophy of Christian faith.

2.   We must be willing for them, in certain areas of life, to choose freely among various options, even if they do not choose as we would prefer.

3.   We must allow them to experience the natural consequences of their choices, even if those consequences are painful to them and to us.

This process is a difficult one to follow, especially for caring Christian parents—or churches—who strongly believe in their doctrine and deeply love their young people. In a sense, the more passionately we love our children and our church, the more difficult it can be to allow the freedoms which are an important ingredient in teaching them to choose the right path. It requires "tough love" to see a child make a wrong choice, knowing that the consequences of that choice will be painful, on the principle that to do so will be helpful to the child in the long run.

Let's take a closer look at those three principles:

We must allow our children to become aware of the various alternatives to our particular philosophy of Christian faith.

To choose intelligently those things which are good, one must be aware of the bad.   There is a pattern which has been repeated so often that it is almost a cliche: good boy/girl grows up in conservative Christian home/church, always does what is right, never seems to rebel or disobey, then grows up and goes off to college/work/army, seems suddenly to discard his/her walk with the Lord entirely to the utter dismay of everyone back home. (The most common variation on the scenario is one in which it happens earlier, while the child is still living at home.)

Even at Christian colleges, where there is ample opportunity for Christian friends and influences, this pattern sometimes is seen. Very often—though certainly not always—a closer inspection of the child's history reveals that this apparent collapse of parental influence has come at the *first exposure* in the child's life to a lifestyle and worldview different from that of his parents and local church.

It is as if the child is saying, "Oh, wow, I have always done what was right because I didn't know what the options were!" So, like a kid suddenly turned loose in a candy store, the urge to sample everything in sight seems irresistible.

We must be willing for them, in certain areas of life, to choose freely among various options, even if they do not choose as we would prefer.

To truly choose the right path, one must have some knowledge of what the wrong path offers. Accepting the straight and narrow road is only meaningful if one is simultaneously rejecting the broad and easy road, and that requires some knowledge of it.

The Bible refers to Moses as *"choosing* rather to suffer affliction with the people of God, than to enjoy the pleasures of sin for a season" (Hebrews 11:25). He obviously knew not only that sin was an option but that it was a pleasurable option and, furthermore, that its pleasure would endure only for a season. That is virtually a definition of an intelligent moral choice.

If our children are to learn to make intelligent moral choices, we must allow the same elements to be in place: a free choice, accompanied by an awareness of both the upside and the downside of both options.

The upside of sin or disobedience of any type is that it feels good; the downside is that it ultimately destroys the person who engages in it.

The upside of morality and faith is that it produces a happy life and eternal reward; the downside is that it frequently requires self-discipline of the flesh and rejection by other people.

Everyone who decides to follow God should do so recognizing those simple facts, because any other basis will produce a decision which will not last. "Choosing" in the sense of Proverbs 22 requires an awareness of all those options, and that is why the scripture can confidently assure parents that a child who has "chosen the right path" in this manner will not depart from it when he has grown older.

For parents, allowing that process to operate can be frightening. It also can be extremely difficult to know when and how to allow such choices to be made, how much exploration is a healthy part of the process, and how much is premature and unwise. Obviously, a very young child should not be exposed to options for which he is unprepared, nor should he be allowed to choose a path before fully understanding the implications of his choice. But the starting place for all parents must be a commitment, at least in principle, to the necessity of such choice making being allowed.

One important reminder is in order here: Satan is a roaring lion, seeking to devour our children, and he can never be counted on to show them the downside of sin. Satan is a liar, but he often comes dressed as openness personified. He will show our children the pleasures of sin but not that those pleasures last only for a season. We can combat Satan best by being more honest with our children than he is. If we are willing to show them the whole picture, we can best gain credibility and trust with them. If they are able to dismiss us as being dishonest about the pleasures of sin, why should they listen when we warn about its dangers? On the other hand, we must not depend on the world to show them the dark side of sin, because the world will lie to them every time.

Perhaps the parable of Jesus' with which parents can best identify is that of the Prodigal Son. In this story, the father allowed the child to choose the wrong path and allowed him to suffer the consequences, with the final result that the child ultimately chose the right path and did so in a manner that suggested a permanent, lifelong commitment to it. Trying to be such a parent, knowing when to force a certain kind of behavior and when to allow another, knowing whether a child can handle the pressure of negative influences in a constructive way, is extremely difficult for even the best and most skillful parent. It can only be accomplished by the power of the Holy Spirit and through prayer and seeking the mind of Christ.

We must allow them to experience the natural consequences of their choices, even if those consequences are painful to them and to us.

It is possible to avoid the cliche that children "go wild" as soon as they are outside the control of their Christian parents. The key seems to be our ability to provide them with a gradually expanding set of personal choices as they grow older. Gradually we grant them a larger and still larger view of the world in which they will live, showing them that there are choices to be made and letting them practice making some of those choices. In doing so, we try to guarantee that all the information about those choices is available to them. Then comes what is often the hardest part—allowing the natural consequences of their choices to operate, refusing to rescue them too easily and too often from the pain which their bad choices produce, but somehow still being there with a helping hand at the right time.

If this process occurs in a thousand small instances over the course of many years as the child grows from a toddler into a young adult, one can hope that the painful consequences of bad choices will never be fatal or cripplingly severe. That would be, perhaps, every parent's most fervent prayer, and for that we can only trust God.

CHAPTER

4

GOD'S WORD

■

Every local youth program is built on the same four foundation stones. Whatever the size or nature of the congregation, if its youth program does not include these four elements, it does not serve its teenagers well. The four fundamentals of the discipling process are these: knowledge of God's Word, worship and praise, service to the kingdom of God, and a separated lifestyle.

No youth program lacks all four of these elements. Obviously for a youth group to exist at all, something must be occurring among the teenagers which falls into one of these four categories. But it is not at all uncommon for virtually all the time and energy of the program to flow into one or two of these areas, to the exclusion of the others. Such a program may be "successful" in the sense that it attracts large numbers of teenagers. It may be exciting and popular. It may fully meet the expectation of the adults in the church, or even of the pastor. But if it omits an emphasis on any one of these four fundamentals, it is not a well-balanced ministry and to that degree has not served its members well.

Such an imbalance may develop in a variety of ways. Most often it issues from the teenagers' own immature tastes and preferences. Adolescents are no more balanced in their choice of religious activities than they are in choosing food—rarely will they voluntarily eat vegetables and nutritious meals as long as a McDonald's or Pizza Hut is open. Similarly, they will attempt to survive on the spiritual equivalent of junk food and dessert if allowed to do so. Given a choice of a pop-style Christian concert or a solid Bible study, most teenagers will choose the concert. Parents and youth workers should not be discouraged by this pattern, even when found among older and more spiritually established teenagers. It is a natural part of adolescent life and does not mean the kids are failing to grow spiritually as they should.

But while youth leaders should not view such preferences as abnormal, they should yet not allow the program to be set by the immaturity of the teens. What kids prefer is not necessarily what kids need; providing balance is the responsibility of adult leaders.

Another major source of imbalance among the four components of the youth program is the tendency of a youth program to reflect the basic style and values of the larger congregation of which it is a part. In short, many youth programs are out of balance because the local church program itself is out of balance. If the agenda of the congregation does not include an emphasis on biblical holiness, for example, then it is highly unlikely that the youth group will emphasize it. A congregation which is unable to participate fully in open expressions of praise and worship will not often consider that to be an important part of the training of its young people. When adult Christians ignore the mandate for service to others, their children and grandchildren will be unlikely to give it much attention. It has been said that a youth group cannot be very much better than the church which sponsors it, and that is certainly true of the balance of its discipleship training.

The first component of a good youth program is an emphasis on the knowledge of God's Word. This is an almost purely educational function; it can be achieved by a combination of Sunday school, mid-week Bible study and preaching in the Sunday worship services. Although the supplement of special programming can sometimes be valuable, it is not necessary if the traditional times of teaching are well-utilized.

Teenagers need to learn what is in God's Word. They need to hear Bible stories, even the familiar ones they have heard over and over since childhood. They need to learn the basic doctrines of the church, including elementary theological vocabulary and concepts. A Christian 18-year-old who has grown up in the church and yet cannot offer an informal definition of *justification* is an indictment of the congregation which produced him. In my years at Lee College, I have been amazed at the level of biblical and spiritual illiteracy which exists among so many of the Church of God young people who come to us as freshmen. In many cases, teenagers arrive at college age having sung in teen choirs, attended youth camps and had their hands held by full-time youth pastors throughout their entire teen years—but who still have practically no specific knowledge of the Bible and basic doctrine.

Why do we tolerate such a lower level of awareness of the Bible than of every other major area of learning? Why do we insist that kids learn the multiplication tables and how to diagram a complex sentence but not that they learn what an epistle is? A church that spends great effort and energy to entertain its young people, or takes pride in the manner in which they are included in its worship, or maintains strict requirements in the way they dress or behave, but does not invest equally in their knowledge of the Bible is dangerously omitting the most basic component of all.

One of the admirable qualities of the Roman Catholic Church over the centuries has been its commitment to teaching its doctrine to its young people—whether they want to learn it or not. Some

Pentecostal version of the Catholics' traditional cate-chism classes would be an innovation that would serve us well. Our tendency has been to so stress the importance of the heartfelt experience that we some-times forget that all such experience issues ulti-mately from a knowledge and acceptance of God's Word.

Too often the Sunday school hour is frittered away in an attempt to address "relevant issues," the midweek Bible study hour gets preempted by films and music and special programs, and Sunday nights are given over to choir practice and testimony time. The result is that a teenager in a well-organized local church can literally grow up without ever being taught what is *in* the Bible on which he is challenged to build his life!

WORSHIP AND PRAISE

■

The second component of balanced discipling is training in worship and praise.

The worship of Almighty God is both instinctive and learned. On the one hand, it issues naturally from a heart that is warmed by the presence of God. On the other hand, we must be taught how to express those Godward feelings, and especially how to do so in a disciplined way (in our private devotions) and in an orderly way (in our public worship).

The spontaneity and naturalness of praising God is one of the most beautiful evidences that we were indeed made in His image. A poignant story told by Charles Colson in his book *Born Again* illustrates this. Colson describes an event which occurred before his conversion to Christ, at a time when he called himself an agnostic:

"I found myself remembering a curious shining moment seven years before. In the summer of 1966 I had bought a 14-foot sailboat for my two boys and hauled it to a friend's home on a lake in New Hampshire to teach them to sail. My son, then ten, was so excited over having his own boat that even though a gentle summer rain was falling the day of our arrival, he was determined to try it out.

"As the craft edged away from the dock, the only sound was the rippling of water under the hull and flapping of the sail when puffs of wind fell from it. I was in the stern watching the tiller, Chris in the center, dressed in an orange slicker, holding the sheet. As he realized that he was controlling the boat, the most marvelous look came over his cherubic face, the joy of new discovery in his eyes, the thrill of feeling the wind's power in his hands. I found myself in that one unforgettable moment quietly talking to God. I can even recall the precise words: 'Thank you, God, for giving me this son, for giving me this wonderful moment. Just looking into this boy's eyes fulfills my life. Whatever happens in the future, even if I die tomorrow, my life is complete and full. Thank you.'

"Afterwards, I had been startled when I realized that I had spoken to God, since my mind did not assent to His existence as a Person. It had been a spontaneous expression of gratitude that simply bypassed the mind and took for granted what reason had never shown me. More—it assumed that personal communication with this unproven God was possible. Why else would I have spoken unless deep down I felt that Someone, somewhere, was listening?"

That innate impulse to express oneself to God is in all of us, lying just beneath the surface of our various personalities and culture-bound habits. It lies there in the heart of every teenager, ready to be tapped and formed. It is the task of the church to teach teenagers how to use it, how to glorify God and enrich themselves spiritually by its full expression.

The heavy emphasis on worship and praise which has marked the Charismatic renewal is perhaps the greatest gift of that movement to the larger body of the church. It is true that the mainstream Pentecostal church has a rich and wonderful worship tradition all its own; in fact, it was our insistence on free full-gospel worship which most dramatically set us apart from the old Protestant denominations. But in the Pentecostal churches, as in all others, there is constant need for revitalization in worship, and the very richness of our tradition can itself become an obstacle to that freshness. It is not enough that young people worship along with the rest of the congregation; they must be taught about worship, be led to discuss it and understand it, and be encouraged to participate in more and more personal ways. The deadliest habit into which teenagers fall so readily is that of being spectators at the worship of others. Their tendency to sit together in an informal "teen ghetto" in a particular part (usually the rear) of the sanctuary lends itself to this pattern. It is too easy for young people to feel that if a worship experience is not designed specifically *for* them and organized *around* them, they are not obliged to have anything to do with it at all, except as passive spectators.

This chronic problem is best addressed in the youth group itself, not in the general worship service. The youth leader must make it a priority and put his personal clout on the line if necessary to prod the teenagers constantly in this direction. It is one of the problems which is difficult for parents to solve. It can only be dealt with effectively on the positive basis of worship involvement, not as a discipline problem or a simple matter of territorial rule making (*i.e.*, "No, Junior, you may *not* sit on the back row again!"). This is one of those areas in which a good offense is the best defense.

In addition to the concerns of public worship, it is the responsibility of a local church to lead its young people to develop private worship patterns of disciplined prayer and Bible reading. It is not enough to preach about prayer and Bible reading or to *tell* kids how important such a devotional life is. As in so many areas, youngsters need to be taught *how*, not merely *why*, they should go about it. A creative youth leader can devise ways of helping kids get started—crutches, if you will—with the practice of a regular devotional life. The effort will never end, of course. This is one part of the youth director's work which requires continual work; discipline in private devotions is one of the most difficult traits for a Christian of any age to develop, and the youth leader must show the way over and over again.

Last year as spring break approached at Lee College, I was burdened about this problem of prayer and Bible reading among our students. In a chapel service the week before the break, I asked our students how many of them would volunteer to join me in a weeklong commitment to private worship wherever they happened to be during the holiday. Over 800 students signed pledge cards to do so.

I wrote a special six-day guide for prayer and Bible reading that was specifically tied to the concerns and needs of Lee students and mailed them to the addresses provided by the 800 participants. That week, in a variety of settings all across the country, we all knew we were reading the same Scripture passages, praying for the same needs and bearing the same burdens to the Lord. Even before the week was over, I began receiving positive reports from students. The whole experience turned out to be profoundly meaningful for many of them. In my years at Lee, nothing has produced such a response as that simple six-day experience in private worship.

I recount this because it illustrates what I mean by creative leadership in this area—showing, rather than just telling—devising some small way to instill the principle of private worship. Obviously, every one of those 800 students had been told many times over that Bible reading and prayer are important. All of them already had good intentions in that respect; probably many of them would have done what they did over spring break without my encouragement. But by taking a brief, manageable time period, giving a focus on the combined effort we would share together, and "making it easy" by writing the guide and mailing it to them, we raised the awareness of many students about their devotional life. We made the point. Kids who otherwise would not have done so participated in these devotions. That is the way, bit by bit, teenagers grow into disciples.

An initiative similar to this can be led by any parent or youth leader, with one teenager or a hundred, at almost any time. The details will vary, and one time will not be enough. But that is one of the ways we can go about teaching this important priority of the Christian life.

6

SERVICE

■

The third foundation of discipleship is service.

No Christian's life is complete without service to God and others. For a young person as surely as for the oldest veteran of the church, a willingness to serve is a necessary part of full discipleship.

Both the impulse to worship God and the impulse to serve Him arise from the work of the Holy Spirit in the believer's life. For most of us who were reared in the Pentecostal tradition, opportunities to worship came immediately and frequently after our conversion. Barely do we stand up from the prayer of repentance before we are taught and encouraged to express our impulse to worship the God who has saved us. It is as natural as breathing.

Equally as natural is the spiritual desire to serve. In a sense, service to God is the way we act out those emotions of praise and gratitude which we verbally—or even physically—express in worship. Having been so greatly blessed by God, we arise to *do something* in return, to place ourselves at the service of this God.

Dr. Mark Rutland, an extraordinary young preacher who is associate pastor at the Mount Paran Church of God in Atlanta, tells of an experience in which he saw a young child fall into a motel swimming pool. The child had been briefly left unattended by his parents and fell into the pool. Mark happened to be there at the right time and rescued the child from almost certain drowning. When the father of the child rushed to the poolside to see what had happened, he literally fell to his knees before Mark, so emotionally did he express his thanks.

"I'll never forget the look of total and complete humility, the posture of gratitude, when he realized I had saved his child. He almost literally prostrated himself in front of me and begged, 'Is there anything I can do to show you how much I appreciate what you have done for me?' "

Here was someone who had been given a great gift—the gift of his child's life—by the action of a total stranger, and his feeling of gratitude was so strong that he naturally wanted to do something *for* Mark to express it.

That is the impulse toward God which is evoked from men and women who realize how great is the gift of life that God has so freely given them. Our shouts of joy and worship should be followed by acts of service, and it is the task of the church to teach young people this natural connection.

We do not work for God just because He needs us or because others need Him. We engage in the service of God because it is the only appropriate way to respond to what He has already done for us.

How do we serve God? By serving others. It is one of the simplest and clearest truths of Scripture:

'For I was hungry and you gave me something to eat, I was thirsty and you gave me something to drink, I was a stranger and you invited me in, I needed clothes and you clothed me, I was sick and you looked after me, I was in prison and you came to visit me.'

"Then the righteous will answer him. 'Lord, when did we see you hungry and feed you, or thirsty and give you something to drink? When did we see you a stranger and invite you in, or needing clothes and clothe you? When did we see you sick or in prison and go to visit you?'

"The King will reply, 'I tell you the truth, whatever you did for one of the least of these brothers of mine, you did for me' " (Matthew 25:35-40, *NIV*).

Unfortunately, a tendency among many Pentecostals and Charismatics has been to regard our spiritual tradition as one of worship in contrast to the tradition of the mainline denominations, which we see as overemphasizing the "social gospel" and service to other people. This is a dangerous and unnecessary distortion of the demands of Christ, which conveniently lets us off the hook in our social responsibilities. Whether or not older denominations have neglected heartfelt worship and holy living is a separate issue entirely; it in no way reduces our individual mandate from Jesus Christ to offer the cup of cool water in His name.

It is true, of course, that the church is far more than a food bank, a relief agency, an educational system or a recreation center. But is it possible that we have been so determined not to substitute service for true spirituality that we have ignored service almost altogether?

In some congregations, and in some families, it is possible that we have done so. To whatever extent we do, we virtually guarantee that we will raise a generation of spiritual ingrates. It is a sure way of producing young Christians who see the church as a candy store and Jesus as Santa Claus. This generation has been called the "gimme generation," and that tendency is as great in the church as it is outside. Some youth groups' theme might well be "What Have You Done for Me Lately?" We have been so afraid we would lose our young people that we have offered them a church life so easy, so free of demands, so oriented around *their* needs and *their* problems that they have no concept of Christian living as "the way of the Cross."

What is the solution? Offering a steady stream of opportunities to serve, a youth program which gives young people work to do, which teaches them that the greatest joy in life comes not when we receive but when we give. The solution to teenage ingratitude is to create habits of service based on the solid theological groundwork of Matthew 25:35-40.

However one regards his politics, there is no doubt that President John F. Kennedy captured the imagination of America's young people in the early 1960s with his theme of service and hard work. "Ask not what your country can do for you; ask rather what you can do for your country." He challenged them to put a man on the moon, offered hard work in faraway places in the Peace Corps, and generally proposed that there was more to life than the materialism and creature comforts which had so dominated the attention of the nation in the postwar 1950s.

There is something to be learned here. The most effective way to draw young people from the lap of luxury is not to offer more luxury but instead to point them to a higher form of satisfaction—that of service freely given to a noble cause. This is a lesson easily forgotten by an upwardly mobile church like the Church of God, which is emerging from humble origins into that great velvet-lined trap called the middle class. It is easy for all of us, so freshly come from the backside of the tracks, to be too aware of the many things we have which our parents did not have and subtly bequeath that preoccupation to our children.

We must find ways to show our children that the heart of the gospel is getting *nothing* for *something*; it is giving up what you have for the cause; it is bypassing the secular rewards of personal achievement to gain the intangible rewards of service to God and His children. We must teach them that the greatest good is the service of the Kingdom—not for the sake of the Kingdom but for their own sakes. We teach them to serve not because God needs their labor but because they need this fundamental principle as an organizing reality for their lives.

Young people can serve many ways. As a practical matter, teenagers find it difficult to serve those adults in the age bracket of their parents. For some reason, they find it easier to participate in meaningful projects which serve those people substantially older (senior citizens) or younger (children) than themselves. There are plenty of such people in any local church or community. The effective youth leader seeks ways for his teenagers in organized and frequent projects to do things for them.

At Mount Paran our teenagers did their full share of fun and games. Often when we had work projects, such as the typical car washes and bake sales, the purpose was to raise money for our own activities. The most rewarding such project we had, however, was one in which every dime was sent to someone else. A young pastor in South Georgia had a fire in his parsonage in which his family lost virtually all their clothing and other belongings. I told the teenagers about it and challenged them to give up the next weekend to raise money to send to the pastor's family as a gift. They agreed to do so. I never saw them work harder, and at the end of the week, we had earned several hundred dollars, which we sent, unsolicited and unannounced, to this young pastor.

These were kids who could easily have asked their parents to write a few big checks for this cause. The money would have been the same. But in the act of earning it themselves, they achieved something as important as the money, and they definitely realized the difference. *They* cared, so *they* did something about it . . . in Jesus' name. Not Dad. Not Mom. Not the pastor, with a big offering. With their own sweat and effort they made the bucks—and then they gave it all away! That is a pretty powerful feeling. Somehow, when they prayed for God to help that family in their crisis, the prayers had a greater authenticity than would have been possible otherwise.

What is the difference between *service* and *ministry*? The basis for it and the enablement of it.

If I feed a man who is hungry because it is my

duty, that is merely service.

If I feed him because to do so will win me favor or votes or a reputation for good works, that is opportunism.

But if I feed him because in him I see the broken body of Christ, whom I love because He so loved me, and I feed that stranger as if he were Jesus himself, then that is *ministry*, and it will be energized by the power of the Holy Spirit.

That is what a disciple does.

7

A SEPARATED LIFE

■

The fourth basic element of discipling young people is helping them to develop a lifestyle of separation from the world that is based on a biblical concept of holiness.

The tendency toward worldliness, which is by definition simply being like the world, is a problem for Christians of all ages. The pressure to be like the world is particularly linked to a specific period of life—adolescence. "Peer pressure" is a phrase that was coined in recent generations by developmental psychologists, but the phrase is little more than another way of expressing the forces that conspire to make us want to be like the world. Because the teenage years are conspicuous for their pressure toward peer conformity, they are in turn the period when it is most difficult to live in a biblically separated fashion.

The role of the church during this crisis is not that of a moral cop, enforcing the letter of the law for the sake of the law, but that of a moral teacher, helping the teenager to understand the principle of biblical separation and to commit to that principle because it is a requirement of God's Word. If we can accomplish that, the details will fall into place as a logical result.

Of the four basic components of the local church ministry, this is the one which has provided the greatest amount of intergenerational friction throughout the history of our denomination. Young people frequently fail to meet the expectations of adults in the areas of worship, theology and service, but rarely do these disagreements produce the strife, emotional rifts and even bitterness that can accompany the debate over which specific behaviors constitute a truly separated lifestyle.

The tension does not issue from a disagreement over the biblical principle itself but over how it is practiced. For that reason, a good place to start is by teaching young people the principle rather than the specifics rules. No parent or local church can be prepared to specify the rightness and wrongness of every behavior their young people will contemplate in a lifetime. We can never create such a set of guidelines and offer it as a moral absolute. It should be instructive to us that even the Bible itself does not attempt to offer such an exhaustive, detailed approach to a life of holy living. Rather, God offers us the principles and promises to help us apply them in our own personal decisions if we seek His help and follow it conscientiously.

A church must have rules, just as any other institution must. Those rules must be respected, just as the rules of a family and home must be. But for individuals to allow such a set of rules to take the place of the Bible or of the individual's own God-given conscience is to start down a slippery slope indeed.

A healthy, functioning church must include members who are able to make coherent moral decisions based on God's Word in a complex society with many subtle shades of gray. How might the church best produce such Christians?

Children who grow up with an inflexible set of moral values already laid out neatly for them have difficulty making moral judgments on their own later in life. They learn how to respond to authority but not how to weigh a moral decision. They suffer from moral and intellectual malnutrition. It is unreasonable to expect them to bring sensitivity and depth to the moral questions they face as adults. A God-given conscience and intuitive morality provide a starting point for one's individual sense of right and wrong; but, in many respects, the ability to make sound moral judgments is an acquired skill.

If this ability is *not* acquired, it is absent; and the individual moves through life responding not to the *content* of moral arguments but to the level of authority he perceives in the person or institution who offers a particular moral position to him. Most of his decisions in life will be decisions not about right and wrong at all but about how he will respond to authority. He is told what is right and decides only whether to accept or reject that authoritarian judgment based often on factors other than the moral issue itself.

Ideally, then, a church optimizes the moral development of its members by creating an atmosphere of open discussion, interchange of ideas, an opportunity to probe and analyze the moral implications of individual behaviors. The church, particularly one with a solid 100-year history such as the Church of God, should be confident enough of its posture on various moral issues that it can freely encourage dialogue and intellectual exploration. By teaching its members to stretch their muscles in the moral arena, the church helps them acquire the ability to make mature moral judgments. They are learning not just a specific set of moral rules but how to respond to the moral implications of all types of situations as they arise throughout life.

On the other hand, a church that does not provide such experiences for its members impedes their moral development. The individual learns to forfeit his moral decision making to the authority of the church itself, accepting its prescriptions at face value and never fully developing his own personal moral code.

To the degree that the Church of God, or any church, inhibits the development of moral reasoning in its members, it might be said that it prepares them to be good members of the narrow and increasingly irrelevant social institution but prepares them quite poorly to be responsible citizens of the kingdom of God.

A critical question for the church is whether our mission is to teach members how to make sound and scriptural moral decisions or, rather, to deliver to them a fully developed, finished product, some ultimate and comprehensive code. If we have such a code to deliver, our task is that of propagandists and indoctrinators and our efforts should focus on how best to inculcate what we already "know" to be true. If so, we need not be concerned with our members' ability to weigh and interpret the unique, personal elements of their own lives but need only be concerned with how best to bring them into conformity with the code.

The problem with such an approach is that no set of behavioral guidelines is wholly adequate. There simply is no overarching code which covers all eventualities. Even the system of informal rules to which Church of God members currently subscribe is a product of a hundred years of evolution and change. At one time in our history, the drinking of

Coca-Cola was considered a sign of moral weakness, and the general overseer at that time went on record to say so. More recently, wearing a wedding band was officially regarded as the moral equivalent of any other use of jewelry. By majority vote this position was reversed, and wedding bands are now officially judged to be morally safe. Dozens of other informal rules have shifted over the years, and the men and women who provoked those shifts were either villains or heroes, depending on which side they voted. Obviously, a code which is subject to such constant alteration is not carved in granite and should not be treated as such. It is the tendency of institutions to regard past changes as "progress" and potential future changes as "compromise." It is morally arrogant to assume that we have finally arrived at the ultimate combination of behavioral guidelines for contemporary Christians. A sovereign God, in His ultimate authority, declares certain moral absolutes which never vary; but outside these absolute requirements of Scripture, specific moral positions are always, by nature, interpretive. That is an inescapable reality which has frustrated moral absolutists in every generation.

The most compelling reason for helping Church of God members to develop their own moral judgment, then, is that to do so respects the individuality of the believer and prepares him to make the vast number of moral decisions which the church cannot possibly supervise. A more pragmatic argument against the Big Brother approach to morality is that it simply does not work. Seeking to control undesirable behavior by declaring it wrong when the evidence for such a prohibition is not clear in Scripture often results in more, not less, of that behavior.

As an example, consider the case of attendance at movie theaters. When I first began to meet a wide spectrum of Christian teenagers as a student at Lee College in 1965, I was impressed with how many of them went to movie theaters and, even more so, struck by the random fashion in which they decided *which* movies to see. This pattern still exists among older teenagers and young adults from conservative Christian homes: it is not that they attend movies at all but the *promiscuity* with which they attend that is striking. An R-rated film is as likely to be chosen as a less offensive one. Having been told categorically that movies are sinful and having rejected that judgment as incorrect, these young people are left with no guidance or training in how to make intelligent Christian distinctions between good movies and bad ones. A church, by staking out an absolutist position, in effect abdicates its responsibility in this area. By attempting, and in large measure failing, to convince its members that *all* movies are bad, the church undercuts its ability to address the issue at all. Rather than producing a nonmoviegoing generation, a church instead produces large numbers of indiscriminate moviegoers who do not evaluate their choice of movies in moral terms at all.

So by overreaching in this fashion, the church achieves a result opposite that which it intends. More importantly, the church suffers a damaging loss of credibility by refusing to reassess its position, which a changing technology (*e.g.*, television, videotape players, cable, hotel-room HBO) has made increasingly untenable.

The point of this example is not to address the question of movie attendance itself but rather to illustrate the hazards of taking an all-or-nothing position on any practice which is morally ambiguous. The same point might be made about many other issues on which the church has passed judgment. In each case the outcome for the church is not just loss of control on the particular practice in question but a weakening of the entire structure of moral leadership among its members. A member who in good faith concludes that his church has taught him incorrectly in one matter finds it easier to reach the same conclusion about a different matter. Psychologists call this the "spread of effect." If the church's moral vision is not to be trusted in the matter of movies, might not its judgments on divorce, abortion, sexual behavior or gambling also be suspect? That is the question asked when the church claims moral ground which it cannot defend.

It should be observed at this point that one of the most important functions of the church is to proclaim "Thus saith the Lord" to a confused world. This prophetic role should not be minimized. The greater danger, however, is not that the church neglects to speak in this fashion but that it does so with such little care that the impact of its message is lost. Too often we begin a statement with "Thus saith the Lord" and proceed to ad-lib the rest of the paragraph. Having declared that it speaks for God, the church has a responsibility to ascribe to Him only that body of revealed truth of which it is absolutely certain. Certain unyielding imperatives *do* exist, and the church should not be reluctant to say so. The clarity of some scriptural demands is such that little room is left for individual interpretation. It would be foolish for the church to agonize over the moral implications of adultery, theft, murder or lying, for example. In such cases, we can confidently declare, "Thus saith the Lord."

Sometimes, however, a church goes beyond that firm biblical ground and dares to preface its own biases with "Thus saith the Lord." At that point it loses credibility, first with the outside world and then with its own members. The church fritters away its moral capital on matters of dubious importance. The currency is debased. The moral authority of the church, which is its most valuable property, is gradually eroded, and its moral preachments are simply not respected—not even by its own people. A church—or a minister—must know when to express an attitude with "Thus said the Lord" and when instead to use the more modest preface "It seems to me . . . . "

Would it not be better to claim divine authority for only the most basic scriptural rules and teach church members to work out the details of their own daily walk with God for themselves? It would seem so.

Our role as the church is to teach biblical moral values, and beyond that, the actual, ongoing behavior which those moral decisions generate. We are concerned not only with the refinement of a person's moral thought but with what he does about it. We are not satisfied simply that men and women *know* what is right but that they *do* what they know to be right. Further, we believe in a God who can produce in an individual that change of heart and behavior which makes possible a truly moral life.

THE ROLES OF
THE MINISTERS

■

A few churches have the size and resources to hire a full-time or part-time youth pastor whose job it is to develop and lead a complete program for the young people of the congregation. More commonly, a committed lay member serves that same function on a volunteer basis.

In either case, however, the key to the local church's ministry to its young people is the pastor. As the spiritual leader of the congregation, he must always be the person who bears the primary responsibility for ministry to the young people, as to all other constituents in the congregation.

No matter how many youth specialists may be hired by a local church, there can be no substitute for a senior pastor who is sensitive to the needs of his young people and ministers effectively to them. Though youth leaders bear the responsibility for frontline contact with the teenagers, they achieve the best results when they see their job as that of bringing kids into a positive relationship with the church, making it possible for the senior pastor to minister to them on a regular basis.

A pastor can never delegate his job of ministry to the youth in his congregation. It is a responsibility that can never be farmed out to a younger minister or staff member. What *can* be delegated is the daily contact with them, the nuts and bolts of operating the total scope of their church activities, and the task of bringing greater numbers of them into the life of the church itself. But when those duties are being performed by the youth leader, the spiritual responsibility for knowing who they are and taking them and their needs before the Lord on a regular basis must always be accepted by the pastor himself.

This is not to say that the youth leader is merely a technician who directs traffic and mixes up the Kool-Aid while the pastor provides all the spiritual nurture. Far from it. The youth leader is a minister, not merely an activities coordinator, and should feel the weight of his own priestly role as well. But he must never be expected to bear it alone. His ministry is best seen as a partnership with the senior pastor for a specific part of the flock.

There are two extremes to be avoided. In one case, the pastor (and other congregational leaders) feels the teenagers are someone else's specific responsibility, so they don't have to worry about it very much. In the other extreme, the pastor fails to take the youth minister seriously as a spiritual leader, regarding him instead as something of a fun-and-games specialist.

In the ideal situation, the pastor would trust the youth minister's own spiritual vision and maturity in ministering to young people but would not leave it up to him entirely. Rather, he would depend on the youth minister to feed him information and suggestions that would enable him as senior pastor to minister to them in a more effective and personal way.

Here is a brief set of suggestions which might address this critically important, triangular relationship between senior pastor, youth leader (whether a paid staff minister or a volunteer member of the congregation) and parents:

1. The youth leader must actively work to enhance the standing of the pastor with his teenagers.

This is more than a suggestion; it is a rule that should be carved in granite somewhere. There is no shortcoming of a pastor so grave that it entitles the youth minister to be critical of him to the congregation. There can be only one leader in the local church, and that is the pastor. As long as he is the pastor, he deserves the full support of his staff. A staff associate who feels unable to give his boss that kind of positive support has a moral obligation to leave and find a pastor who can inspire his full confidence.

God does not bless disloyalty and treachery. To the contrary, there is considerable evidence in Scripture that God places authority in the church and requires obedience to that authority.

There is a natural competition which can develop very easily between a pastor and his youth leader. The reason for having a specialist in youth ministry is that teenagers do comprise a distinctive subset of the general church population, and as such they have a different approach to many things, such as dress, music, vocabulary and entertainment. The effective youth minister will usually be much more attuned to this distinctive teen subculture than the senior pastor will be. Also, as a result of the intense personal interaction within an active youth group, the young people will develop a much closer personal attachment to the youth minister than to the pastor in most cases.

It can be tempting for the youth leader to exploit his popularity and intimacy with the teenagers and their families in an effort, sometimes even unconsciously, to establish his own following within the congregation. The pastor, usually an older man and often preoccupied with matters other than teenagers, is an easy target for the youth minister who becomes a cheap-shot artist. If the youth minister is not careful, he begins to take pleasure in his image as more hip, more fun and more caring than the pastor and is tempted to underscore the contrast rather than to minimize it.

When a youth minister begins to enjoy, even subtly, the image of the pastor as a rather square, out-of-touch old guy who can't possibly understand teenagers as well as he can, the youth minister is encouraging a competitive situation which can only be bad for all concerned. One of the first items on every youth minister's priority list should be an active, ongoing effort to build up the pastor, to make him look good, to create the most positive attitude possible toward the pastor by the teens and their families.

There is no more constructive role the youth minister can play than that of making the pastor a hero to his teenagers so that when the pastor walks to the pulpit to preach every Sunday, the kids are eager to listen. The smart youth leader will use his personal popularity to enhance the pastor's standing with the congregation.

2. **The pastor must provide a basis for the youth minister's role as a spiritual leader**.

The youth minister's support of the pastor must be reciprocated, of course, if the team is to be optimally effective. Whereas the senior pastor's greatest need with teenagers in his congregation is to be seen as caring, in tune and relevant to their particular needs, the youth minister's greatest need is to be taken seriously by the congregation at large as a leader with a certain moral authority and spiritual substance.

No one can help the youth minister with this need more effectively than the senior pastor. In fact, in most congregations the pastor can absolutely bestow or withhold such standing upon a youth leader. In almost any case, it is impossible for the youth minister to be taken seriously by the congregation if the pastor does not do so and does not communicate it in a public way.

One of the important ways the pastor can achieve this is simply by inviting the youth minister to fill the pulpit on a frequent basis—not just for special youth emphasis services but for regular worship services in which he can address the spiritual needs of the entire congregation. Obviously, the degree to which this can be done depends largely on the preaching ability of the youth minister himself, but it should be regarded as a goal in any case.

In a church, all authority must issue from moral and spiritual authority. It is impossible for a youth minister to rise higher in the esteem of the congregation than his personal level of spiritual and moral maturity. It is a common mistake for young ministers, especially those who are barely adults themselves, to build a following among the members based solely on their personal charisma, youthfulness and rapport with the kids. This can become a trap, however, as the youth minister becomes older and more established in his work. The fun-and-games image which he has developed can impede his efforts to gain the full respect of the congregation as a man of God and a leader of depth and substance.

In short, the pastor and youth minister must work together to help gain the congregation's respect for the youth leader as a spiritual leader. The pastor, by sending the wrong signal to the worshipers or the youth minister and by failing to take responsibility for a congregationwide vision, can sabotage that effort.

3. Parents must lend support to the youth program as well as to the youth director.

In most situations, parents of teenagers are older and more experienced adults than the director of their church youth program. A typical situation finds 40-year-old parents of teenagers entrusting the care of their children to the hands of 25-year-old youth ministers. It is only natural that they should do so with a certain amount of misgiving: "I sure hope that young fella knows what he's doing!"

The smart parent will try to avoid communicating to the child whatever lack of confidence he feels in the youth director. If a youth pastor gives a teenager lots of time, love, prayer and personal attention, the positive impact can far outweigh whatever small mistakes in leadership he may commit. The parent is best advised, even when he does not agree with a particular part of the youth director's agenda or philosophy, to be patient, to pray for the young people *and* their leader, and to try to find indirect ways of influencing the situation positively.

It is important for parents to remember that the youth leader is often himself young and in the process of developing a mature philosophy of discipleship. Rather than expecting too much of him or being too quick to criticize his decisions or style, the parent should see the youth leader's immaturity as an opportunity for the parent as an older Christian to support and encourage—and even help to shape—a hardworking younger Christian.

Some adults who would not dream of criticizing or attacking their senior pastor act as if a youth pastor is fair game. To the contrary, it is the youth pastor who is particularly in need of the congregation's support.

This support is expressed not just by withholding criticism but by actively seeking tangible ways to contribute to his efforts. In a local youth ministry there are never enough volunteers, dollars or hours to get the job done. Parents who step forward with an offer to help—whether with labor, money or in other ways—not only gain a friend in their youth pastor but also send a message to their children that they care enough to get involved.

VOLLEYBALL AS A SPIRITUAL EVENT

■

One of the most persistent problems faced by a youth pastor is that he usually has very few ways of controlling the behavior of the young people under his supervision.

Fortunately, this problem is not a serious one in his relationship with the majority of the members in a typical youth group. But virtually every church youth group includes one or two teens who require the imposition of discipline lest they disrupt the activity of the entire group. Even the "good" kids in any group occasionally behave badly, either in outright violation of the group's rules or by simply deciding not to do what the leader wants them to do.

By their nature adolescents need constant control, and the local church is an institution that possesses very few mechanisms by which the youth leader can maintain that control. To illustrate, consider what a sharp contrast is seen in the school, the other social institution where teenagers operate in concentrated numbers for extended periods of time.

A high school or junior high school has several effective ways of controlling teen behavior. First, there is the simple device of grades. Any teacher in an individual classroom can punish bad behavior, or the absence of positive behavior, by giving bad grades. A second device is the imposition of outright punishment in various forms, ranging all the way from the old-fashioned paddling—now banned in many school systems—to sentencing the child to spend after-school hours in detention hall to requiring extra work assignments. A third control mechanism available to schools is the simple, if extreme, matter of expelling students from school altogether or suspending them for a few days, sometimes requiring a review with the principal before readmission.

These three major means by which secondary schools control the behavior of their students all share a common characteristic: they are punitive. They work because the school has the power to make something bad happen in the life of the child.

The church has no such punitive powers. Consider the plight of local church youth leaders. They are dealing with the same teenagers, with the same problems of misbehavior, and are expected to maintain a similar or even higher level of control. But they have at their disposal none of the punishment-based ways of getting their youngsters to act right. They cannot give bad grades, threaten to flunk kids out, assign hours in detention, give extra homework and certainly cannot kick the kids out of church.

Fortunately, there is more than one way to control behavior. There is the carrot as well as the stick. A mule can be made to move forward either by hitting him on the backside with the stick (punishment) or by dangling the juicy carrot in front of his nose (reward). Like the mule, the teenager will respond to either motivational device.

Since youth leaders in churches have no sticks, they must depend heavily on lots of carrots. The only long-term solution to their problem is the creation of a system of rewards which are so desirable that behavior can be controlled by giving or withholding those rewards.

The key word here is *create*. For the most part, rewards will not be readily available in the church situation, so the effective youth leader must find and develop them. If the only way he has of punishing kids for misbehavior is to withhold carrots, then he must have the carrots there to begin with. In other words, the church youth group must include enough positive, fun, attractive features that to miss them is punishment for the teen.

If I were a consultant called into a local church to evaluate its youth program, the first question I would ask is this: "Is it fun? Do the young people usually enjoy themselves and have a good time when they are at this church or in the company of its youth leaders?" If the answer is no, the program does not include enough carrots to enable its leaders to exercise control when they need to do so. All youth groups seem effective during the week after youth camp or immediately following an especially good revival when the kids are fresh from the altar and highly motivated to seek God and behave according to His standards. But if a group is to be consistently effective, month in and month out, it must offer its customers a good value for the expenditure of their time, strictly on the basis of their personal and social needs.

Let me hasten to say that for the church youth ministry, *fun* is not the end but the means to the end. The goal of the church is not to give kids a good time but to give them the gospel. Spiritual values, not social values, are those the church seeks to impart.

But it cannot impart spiritual values to young people who are not there or who, though physically present, are misbehaving so regularly that an atmosphere for teaching and serious discipling does not exist. The youth leader's first task is to produce an overall program so attractive and enjoyable that it gets the kids there, keeps the kids there, and produces adequate control over them while they are there. Only when that is done does the basis for regular spiritual development exist.

What this translates to as a practical matter is lots of programming which is not directly and gloriously "spiritual" in nature. Sports, parties, social events of various types—all are used as *carrots*. To enjoy these goodies, the young person must come to the youth group and act right when he gets there.

The problem the youth director frequently encounters is the criticism that his program is too oriented around social activities and not enough around spiritual ones—all fun and games, not enough substance. This criticism most often comes from older church members but sometimes will come from the parents of the teenagers themselves simply because those parents are so eager to see their children involved in activity of an obviously spiritual nature.

When I became a youth pastor, I arrived to find a group of teenagers who were, for the most part, rather uninterested in church. They participated in relatively small numbers simply because their parents made them come, and they were turned off and uninvolved when they got there. I set out to produce such a variety of interesting activities that it would make kids want to come be a part of it, and that effort was successful; but in the beginning the carrots were mostly social and recreational in nature.

Predictably, I began to hear grumbling from some of the older, more conservative church members. It seemed to them that all I did was "play" with the teenagers. One of the critics observed: "I thought we hired this young fella to be a spiritual leader for our teenagers. . . . What's spiritual about volleyball?"

On one occasion, an older gentleman pulled me aside to offer the comment that he thought the youth group was having too much fun and was not doing enough Christian service. He suggested that I discontinue the Saturday recreational sessions we were having and instead take the kids out on Saturdays to distribute gospel tracts door-to-door. He had done that himself when his son was a youngster, he told me, and recommended it highly. What he failed to mention, and indeed seemed not to make a logical connection, was that his son, now grown, was unsaved, unchurched and totally uninterested in becoming either.

I persisted in building a youth program that included lots of volleyball and pingpong—unspiritual though they were—and other types of social activity. The result was that our youth group soon grew into a very large one, the kids became personally attached to me and my wife and to one another, and most important, *the church became an important focal point of their lives.* Then, but only then, was it possible to begin serious discipling and spiritual training. The preaching and teaching they were hearing, the regular worship experiences with the adult congregation as well as the special worship times just with the youth group, had greater effect on a larger number of kids, and gradually we developed into a cohesive group over which I could exercise very firm control.

To paraphrase an old cliche: The youth group that plays together prays together. And stays together.

Adults who expect their teenagers to spend most of their time together in prayer, worship and the study of Scripture are imposing an unreasonable expectation on the group and its leaders. The inevitable result will be a smaller group with less impact on the lives of its members than would otherwise occur. In such cases, the teenagers are forced to meet their social and recreational needs in other settings, and those settings will often then provide the network of friends and loyalties which will be most important to the child.

In too many churches the youth group becomes a "holy huddle" of a few teenagers where all the activity must be overtly spiritual and the other things in life happen somewhere else. In such cases, sadly, many of the teenagers are simply waiting passively to become old enough to drop out of the church.

Let me repeat: The fun is not the end but the means to the end. Any youth program which emphasizes social activity to the exclusion of teaching, discipleship and service to others misses the mark badly. Young people can and should be taught that witnessing is important and that it can be personally rewarding. They can be taught that there is great satisfaction to be had in serving others. They can be shown that there is a time for seriousness and sobriety, that life is not just one long party.

But in the beginning, there must be an answer to the question which is implicitly asked by every young teenager: "Why should I cooperate? Why should I get involved with this church stuff? Why should I come and do what you want me to do?" And if the only answer to that "Why should I . . . ?" is that he will get in trouble with his parents if he doesn't, then the youth leader has a major problem on his hands.

As a youth pastor, I often visualized the church and its teenagers as a kind of solar system, with the church as a planet and all the teenagers as little satellites orbiting around it. My job was to keep those kids in the orbit of the church, within its gravitational field and influence. So long as they stayed in the orbit of the church, exposed to the preaching of the pastor and the love and influence of the members, within the sound of the gospel in various forms on a regular basis, there would be opportunities for spiritual values to take hold. The tragedy is when the young person leaves the church's orbit altogether and sails off into outer space somewhere. When that happens, it becomes irrelevant— in the life of that particular young person—how good the altar services are, how strong the preaching, how fervent the spiritual climate in that congregation, because he is not there for it to matter at all. His life now revolves around some other planet in some other galaxy. That has been the great tragedy in our churches too many times.

So the youth leader must constantly ask the question "Am I keeping them in the orbit of the church?" If so, something spiritually significant can happen.

Often after too many pizza parties and camping trips, I was tempted, like every youth worker is, to ask myself whether or not it was worth all the effort. *Am I really accomplishing anything of spiritual value with these kids? Where is the ministry in all this? Am I leading these kids to God, or am I just a glorified baby-sitter?* One of the things that kept me going in such times was the model in my head of the church as a planet and the teenagers as constantly revolving around it. My job, I reminded myself, begins with keeping them in the orbit of the church and giving God a chance to keep working on them.

To change the metaphor, remember, Christ himself described us as "fishers of men." What is spiritual about volleyball? Think of it as bait.

DO I HAVE TO GO TO CHURCH?

■

"But, Mom, do I *have* to go to church?"

What parent has not heard that question, or some variation of it, from a teenage child? For churchgoing families, it is a question almost as universally familiar as "How much farther is it?" always heard during long trips in the family car.

The answer to the question almost every time is "Yes, you *do* have to go to church." But knowing the answer doesn't keep the parent from growing very weary of hearing the question from her kids.

It is natural for kids to get tired of going to church, regardless of how good the music and preaching are or how talented the Sunday school teacher. Perhaps no other aspect of Christian child rearing requires such constant discipline as keeping children in church on a regular basis.

Here are a few observations on this most common of all parental problems:

1. With few exceptions, attendance should be required.

Although many parents who read this will be surprised that such a principle should even need to be stated, it is true that the automatic principle of required church attendance for teenagers is breaking down in a surprisingly high percentage of Christian homes. For some reason, parents who would not consider allowing their children to miss school come to regard regular church attendance as an option for their teenagers.

The teenager should know that there are certain things to which the family has made a nonnegotiable commitment, and regular church attendance is one of them. If for no other reason, going to church should be automatic for the sake of communicating this principle.

2. Being in church is good for teenagers, even if they are forced to go.

One of the statements occasionally heard from parents—and certainly from teenagers—is that going to church is not going to do much good if it occurs at the point of a gun, figuratively speaking. This is an interesting argument, but it is not true. One's participation in the process need not be voluntary for it to have a desired effect.

86

At Lee College we have a policy of required attendance at our worship services, three times a week, even though we are dealing not with young teenagers but with collegians whose average age is 20 years old. (This policy is constantly challenged by students, of course, many of them on the basis that their own parents quit making them go to church before they graduated from high school.) I am totally committed to our policy of required chapel attendance, because I have seen over and over during the 18 years I have worked at Lee the impact of worship on the lives of these students, even when they had no choice as to whether or not they would attend.

If there is any single testimony that we at Lee hear more often than any other from our returning alumni, it is that the required chapel attendance policy, burdensome as it seemed at the time, resulted in the transmission of concepts and challenging ideas which remained permanently lodged in the student's experience.

It is true that an unwilling worshiper will not derive as much benefit from a sermon or a song as an enthusiastic worshiper will, but we cannot allow our children to opt out of the process altogether.

3.   A frequent explanation of why the family is committed to regular attendance is helpful.

Though it may not seem so at the time, a child who receives an explanation about such a requirement generally develops more respect for the policy. The answer to the question "Why?" is never "just because," at least not to a child who has reached the teenage years. Occasionally the teenager should be reminded: "We think church attendance is important. We have made a commitment to it. We consider it a part of the discipline of being a Christian. This is one of the ways we express the high value we place on our faith."

Too often, in the rush to get there on time, the parent has little patience with the child's resistance, and going to church is presented as one of those "Shut up and do what I tell you" requirements.

At other times a reason is offered, but it misses the real point of the parent's insistence. A parent often explains why attendance is necessary by saying they will be missed by the pastor, or the crowd is small and they are needed, or in some other way that suggests they are going to church to do someone a favor or meet someone's expectations. Teenagers are more likely to respect the policy if it is consistently explained as a matter of personal conscience and as a matter of a careful policy by which the family expresses its desire to honor the Lord on a regular basis.

Kids who are told they must go to church for the sake of someone else usually wind up resenting both the church and the people whose expectations they are trying to meet by going.

The resentments toward the church which ministers' children so often experience are part of this pattern. It is quite natural for PKs to be told they must go to church because Dad is the pastor and it is therefore expected of them. That may be true, but it is never the primary reason for going. Such an explanation robs the child—indeed, the entire family—of the satisfaction of going to honor God and to express a commitment to Him. It becomes just another part of Dad's job in which they are unwillingly trapped. What do such children do when they are on their own and Dad's job is not relevant to their decision? Usually they drop out of church at a higher rate than laymen's children, all other things being equal.

4. Exceptions should be made, especially as children get older.

There is a certain sense in which the legitimacy of a rule is strengthened by the occasional, judicious granting of an exception to it. If a parent demonstrates a willingness to make exceptions to rules under rare circumstances, the reasonableness of the rule itself, under normal circumstances, is emphasized and validated. (This is not true of a moral or spiritual law, of course. A moral law has its own inherent authority, drawn from Scripture itself, and permits no exception ever, under any circumstances. But the requirement that one must attend every church service does not fall in that category.)

A very young child is more sensitive to habit and pattern than to logic and thus does not benefit in this way from the occasional exception to such a rule. But as children grow into the teenage years, they are seeking evidence of the parent's flexibility in these matters, because such flexibility shows that the parent is sensitive to the person and not just the rules. It is part of a teenager's immaturity to feel that a parent cares more about preserving an abstract principle than about him as a person, about his needs and problems. When the parent is willing on occasion to set aside a rule in order to respond to the teenager's situation, it is an important signal of the parent's priority on the child. The rule serves the child and not vice versa. That is the point which can be made, especially when the rule in question is one that can be safely set aside from time to time, as is the case with church attendance.

When I was a teenager in the late 1950s, I was required by my parents to attend church not only twice each Sunday but also on Wednesday night (prayer meeting) and Friday night (YPE). This was an unarguable policy; we just did it. Period. When I was 13 years old and in the eighth grade, the Mayfield School eighth-grade basketball team, on which I played, entered a tournament at a school across town. We unexpectedly reached the finals of the tournament, to be played on Friday night. Up until that time, I don't recall ever being allowed to miss YPE on Friday night for any reason.

When our team won the semifinals on Thursday night, I faced the humiliating prospect of missing the final game because I was convinced my parents would make me go to church instead. As I headed home from the gym Thursday night, I rehearsed my speech to them—"Please, please, *please* let me play tomorrow night . . . "—but with no enthusiasm, because I had no hope they would even consider it. After all, they were dyed-in-the-wool, fanatic Church of God parents, and what did they really care about me and how badly I wanted to go and how embarrassing it would be to tell the coach I couldn't play?

But I pleaded with them anyway, prepared to be scolded for even asking.

To my utter surprise, they huddled for a few minutes, then told me yes, under the circumstances, they thought it would be all right. Wow! Knock me down with a feather! I could hardly believe it and hustled off to bed before they changed their minds. The next night I went to the tournament, got to play about two minutes at the end of the game and even scored one point on a free throw.

That decision *not* to make me go to church may have been one of the most important decisions my parents made in their entire effort to bring me up as God's child. I doubt that whatever I missed at YPE on that Friday night was important enough to outweigh the enormous value I gained from my parents' decision: a sense that my parents were reasonable, that they cared about how I felt and that their rule about going to church on Friday night was not as important to them as their boy was. It was an insight of incalculable value as I grew older and the tensions between us escalated.

Sometimes, in the imposition of rules, parents unwittingly win the battle and lose the war. This was one of those times in which my parents intuitively understood that a strategic concession would strengthen their hand for more important matters later on.

5. Don't worry that children are unspiritual if they find church unpleasant and boring.

This is an entertainment-oriented, multimedia generation, and it is difficult for a typical Sunday school class or worship service to compete for the attention of a child or teenager. A parent should not be overly concerned at a child's lack of desire to attend church; to kids who are growing up on high-energy television shows and a constant barrage of sophisticated interactive communications techniques, church is likely to be boring at times. The worst thing a parent can do is to overreact by thinking of the child as having a spiritual problem.

A friend of mine in an informal experiment talked to a group of kindergartners who attended the regular adult worship service at the church where their families belonged. He asked them which lasted longer, church or school. Almost without exception they responded that they stayed longer in church, which was actually an hour, than they did in school, where they stayed four hours each day! The point is obvious: One hour sitting on a pew with nothing to do but listen to someone talk *seemed* longer to them than four hours in a rich, interesting kindergarten environment with a variety of things to do and see.

Do you remember Albert Einstein's famous definition of relativity? He said that an hour talking to a pretty girl seems like 10 seconds and 10 seconds sitting on a hot stove seems like an hour. The kindergartners' estimate of their time spent in church is something of the same sort.

11

MAKING A GROUP INTO A TEAM

■

A high priority for every parent—and for leaders of youth groups—is that of creating a cohesive team spirit. A father or mother who can make children feel they are an important part of a team is likely to find that every aspect of behavior management is made easier by a sense of joint effort within the family.

Similarly, youth directors are most effective when they lead in a way that makes their teenagers feel ownership of the goals and activities of the group. This emphasis on team building is what sets cohesive, close-knit youth groups apart from ordinary ones.

The basic rules for team building are the same for the youth group as for the family. In each case, an authority figure sets the agenda and bears the responsibility for the entire unit. In each case, the children and teenagers are a captive audience, to a certain degree, being required to follow the adult whether they gladly accept his leadership or not. The family or youth group that becomes a team is the one in which the attitude is one of positive, enthusiastic acceptance of the leader's priorities and methods.

Although the suggestions which follow are specifically designed for the home, the principles certainly fit a church teen group equally well. Here are a few guidelines by which a *group* can become truly a *team*:

1. Allow your children to participate in making meaningful decisions.

Richard M. DeVos, who is president of one of the nation's leading corporations and is listed by *Forbes* magazine as one of the 400 wealthiest men in the country, is a dedicated father who has reared four children while building his company.

One of the keys to the DeVos paternal style was involving his children, even when they were quite young, in decisions about where the family's philanthropic dollars went. Periodically, he would sit down at the dining-room table with his wife and four children, tell them how much money was available for charitable giving, then place before them the various requests he had received from organizations seeking help.

The DeVos family then made decisions together, with each child, however young, jumping into the discussion to advocate his or her own favorite choice. "These kids are going to grow up with money," DeVos once explained matter-of-factly, "and they may as well be learning how to use it wisely."

Few families have this particular problem, but most have other important decisions which might safely be submitted to family discussion. The choice of vacation sites, how to spend special family evenings, the type of automobile to buy and many other decisions normally made by parents alone can sometimes be made with full family involvement.

It is an axiom in management that people perform better in tasks which they have a hand in choosing. A family or youth group is no different from a corporation in this sense: Children who feel they have ownership of their goals and efforts commit more enthusiastically to them.

2. Give the children as much information as possible about what is happening.

Like any other social organization, a family or youth group thrives on information. The more aware its members are of where the unit is heading and what is coming up next, the better they feel about being a part of it.

Unfortunately, many fathers are particularly poor in sharing goals and future plans with children and often even with their wives. The stereotypic image of the "strong, silent type" of male leadership in which father gives the orders and expects the children to obey trustingly and silently still prevails in too many American homes.

Ring Lardner, the novelist, tells of a conversation which occurred between a father and son as they drove in an automobile through a maze of city streets. The boy suspected that his father may have been lost but was reluctant to suggest such a thing. When finally the boy asked, "Dad, are we lost?" the father responded in classic fashion, "Shut up."

That is the kind of "explanation" many children get from their parents, especially when the family faces a particularly stressful situation. Children ask lots of questions, and answering them with patience and clarity can be tiresome, particularly when the parent is under pressure. We can all identify with the father in the Ring Lardner description; when Dad is already lost and anxious and irritated, the last thing he needs is the persistent questioning of a youngster.

But the parent who tells the children what is going on is usually the parent whose children feel they are on a team. Children can usually be trusted to understand far more than we expect of them. It is easy to condescend to them and to underestimate their ability to join their parents in adult attitudes rather than tell them exactly what the family is facing.

3.   Never miss an opportunity to express pride in what your children accomplish.

This is such an obvious point that it is easy to miss. Parental pride and involvement is the high-octane fuel on which children run, and it is virtually impossible to give them too much of it.

To most children, the parent is the most important scorekeeper. It is the parent who tells the child whether he is a winner or a loser and the parent who invests the child's activities with value by showing interest in him. Few payoffs for accomplishment are more important to children than that of pleasing their parents. No athlete enjoys playing on a team whose coach is impossible to satisfy.

It is a common fear of parents that they will spoil their children if they give too much praise. It is considered bad form to dote on children excessively, and parents often repress the pride they genuinely feel because they fear too much approval will produce a conceited or self-centered child.

Consequently, the natural pride of many parents is held in check, never expressed, and children misread this lack of affirmation as a sign that the parent does not approve of them and their behavior. The impact on the child's self-esteem is predictably negative: "If I can't please my parents, I must not be a very worthwhile person." A parent should remember that children are praise-seeking creatures, and they will usually find an adult somewhere to satisfy their need for self-esteem. The parent who wants his children to feel a part of a family team will make sure he is that adult.

4. Don't be afraid to let your child see your own weaknesses and failures.

Too many parents feel they have to be a superdad or a supermom in order to maintain their child's respect. To the contrary, children want to connect with their parents as flesh-and-blood human beings—not as perfect, invulnerable demigods of some sort. To let children see your own fears and disappointment is a part of letting them "on the team"; it is a way of saying, "I trust you so much that I don't have to be perfect around you."

When a parent tries to fake it, he rarely fools the child anyway. Most children are sensitive to the subtle signs in a parent's mood and body language that says things are not well. They can tell when a parent is anxious or fearful, and to camouflage those emotions signals that the child is not trusted to handle negative information.

Children can be exceptionally sensitive to the true feelings that underlie an adult's professed attitude. A parent who dutifully projects a forced cheeriness, when in reality he is preoccupied with his own fears and anxieties, rarely convinces the child. A parent gains credibility with children, especially as they grow older, if he is willing to be open with them about financial difficulties, job problems, job insecurity, illness and other challenges the family faces.

For the same reasons, it is important to let children know about the parents' own struggles and failures as teenagers and young adults. In talking with college students about their parents, I have been amazed at the number of children who have little knowledge of the humble beginnings and heroic accomplishments of their own parents. Some of the best real-life examples of winning against great odds can be found right in our own homes, and it is a shameful waste for children not to be aware of them.

A father who experienced reverses and disappointments in his early career should not be reluctant, either through a sense of modesty or a hesitancy to appear boastful, to discuss those times with his children. Once we have made it through the tough times, it is tempting to consign the story of our early struggles to the past. We forget that our children see us as having always been the competent, self-confident adults we finally became, and sometimes we prefer that they see us that way.

But the child is cheated when we take that posture. Our children need to know that we were once scared kids ourselves. Once you were self-conscious about your background or your inability to keep up with the other kids in your class or the size of your nose. When a little boy asks his father, "Were you ever scared, Daddy?" he wants the answer to be yes, because he is scared himself sometimes.

5. Find ways to teach your children to support each other, in good times and bad times.

We have discussed the relationship between the parents and the individual children in the family. But another important part of family life is the relationship of the children to each other. If a family is to be a real team, the children must learn to share one another's successes and failures. The lateral relationship among brothers and sisters is just as important as the vertical relationship between children and parents in building a strong sense of the family as a team.

In fact, there are many cases of families with ineffective parents, even abusive parents, in which the children themselves have bound together so tightly as a team that the negative effects of poor parenting were overcome.

Building good relationships among your children requires taking the time and effort for everyone in the family to know what is going on in the life of everyone else. With the full schedules and busy lives most of us lead, that does not come easily. One works at it, or it doesn't happen. It requires parental leadership, or the household fragments into the several separate lives of its members. The home can become little more than a refueling stop for a houseful of virtual strangers who know little about what the others are doing and feeling.

Parents who are team builders use mealtimes, specially designated family evenings, trips in the car and other occasions to listen to one another—not just to be in one another's presence but to listen as the other tells what is happening in his world. This is difficult to do when the television is on or when both teenagers have individual headsets blasting their own music into their ears. People cannot care about one another meaningfully if they do not *know* about one another, and that does not occur through osmosis or just by living under the same roof. It happens when people take time to listen to one another, and that usually happens only when a parent takes the lead.

THE BEST
PARENTAL PATTERN

■

In our attempt to learn how to be parents, we have the best possible teacher in God himself.

Throughout Scripture, God describes Himself as a parent—not just as a father but as a mother as well, on certain occasions. It is this parental style of God which provided the basis of a book called *FatherCare*, which I wrote several years ago. Many other Christian writers and ministers have found the fatherhood of God to offer some very practical lessons in how we ought to relate to our own children.

A good starting place is a familiar parable in which Jesus placed God in the role of the Father and used a son to symbolize all of us:

'There was once a man who had two sons; and the younger said to his father, "Father, give me my share of the property." So he divided his estate

between them. A few days later the younger son turned the whole of his share into cash and left home for a distant country, where he squandered it in reckless living. He had spent it all, when a severe famine fell upon that country and he began to feel the pinch. So he went and attached himself to one of the local landowners, who sent him on to his farm to mind the pigs. He would have been glad to fill his belly with the pods that the pigs were eating; and no one gave him anything.

'Then he came to his senses and said, "How many of my father's paid servants have more food than they can eat, and here am I, starving to death! I will set off and go to my father, and say to him, 'Father, I have sinned, against God and against you; I am no longer fit to be called your son; treat me as one of your paid servants.' " So he set out for his father's house.

'But while he was still a long way off his father saw him, and his heart went out to him. He ran to meet him, flung his arms around him, and kissed him. The son said, "Father I have sinned, against God and against you; I am no longer fit to be called your son." But the father said to his servants, "Quick! fetch a robe, my best one, and put it on him; put a ring on his finger and shoes on his feet. Bring the fatted calf and kill it, and let us have a feast to celebrate the day. For this son of mine was dead and has come back to life; he was lost and is found." And the festivities began' (Luke 15:11-

32, *NEB).*

This parable gives us what is perhaps the best biblical illustration of how we as pastors, youth leaders or parents should properly balance forgiveness with a moral stand against sin. It is not an easy thing to manage. The church must serve the function of both prophet and priest in the world; it must attack sin with prophetic zeal while befriending the sinner with priestly tenderness.

The problem is one of where to place the emphasis. For both a church and a parent, the problem is knowing where one crosses the line from tolerance and forgiveness into outright permissiveness. Or at the other extreme, where does a commitment to righteousness harden into an unloving legalism?

It is, of course, a question of balance, and referring to the parent-child model of God and man throws light on the issue. *In a proper balance, the tilt is emphatically on the side of forgiveness.* In this parable greater value is placed on the human and personal needs of the individual sinner than on the maintenance of a public posture against any particular set of sins. In this moving story, God uses our own parental instincts to show us that human concerns dominate in such cases—it shows that the abstractions of any ecclesiastical code are not as important as expressing love and acceptance to an individual who wants to come home to his father.

We see several aspects of God's fatherliness in

this story. First, we see the degree to which the father is emotionally vulnerable to the child. The child has the power to hurt his father and in this case does so by rejecting him and by living a life contrary to his training. It is his love for the child that makes the father vulnerable. That is always the case with a parent's love: by loving the child, the parent places in the child's hand the power to hurt him. The greater the love, the greater the hurt. That is part of what being a good parent is all about.

One of the toughest parts of my job at Lee College is informing parents that their children have seriously violated rules and are being expelled from school. These are usually Christian parents—good parents—who have sent their child off to a Christian college, only to learn that he or she is in trouble. There is no pain worse than that of a mother or father whose child, having been trusted and loved, disgraces himself. The parents are hurt—partially from their own sense of being betrayed, but mostly for the child they love.

The irony is that the parent hurts because he or she loves. An unconcerned parent feels no pain. By loving the child, the parent renders himself vulnerable to the potential hurt which the child by his behavior produces. That is the nature of parental love, and that is the nature of God's love for us. God is willing to hurt when we stray, if that is the price He must pay for loving us.

A second aspect of God's fatherliness seen in this story is that His is the kind of love which continues regardless of what we do. It is what psychologists call "noncontingent love"—that is, its presence does not depend on our loving in return, behaving in a particular way or anything else. It is just there. It is a part of God's parenthood. We are His children, so He loves us. Period. All the time the Prodigal Son was painting the town, all the time he was making a fool of himself in the big city, all the time he was wallowing in that pigpen, his father was loving him. Nothing he could do could stop his father's love. The father grieved. He stood by the road and hoped to see his son return, and he felt the pain only a parent can feel. But he never quit loving his boy.

To those who proudly erect elaborate hurdles over which people must leap to receive fellowship in God's family, the tale of the Prodigal Son is something of a rebuke. Some natural parents in insisting that their children try to match their ideal model of the perfect child communicate loudly and clearly to the child that he is not loved and accepted as he is but must be virtually perfect in order to be valued. God the Parent does not do this. He gives His love to us as we are—then He points us toward what we can become. His love comes first, not later. It does not depend on our behavior or even on our acceptance of the love itself.

If God is willing to love people as they are and to work on their problems as they go along, certainly the church should be no less accepting. We must not insist that such acceptance and discipline are mutually exclusive expressions of the church; both can and should exist. The question is rather one of priority: What shall the church say first to the individual? The model of parental love shows us that first comes the nurture, then comes the training.

There is in developmental psychology a way of looking at parental styles called the "Schaeffer circumplex model," which suggests that the two major dimensions of parenting are *nurturance* and *control*. Nurturance includes all the parental expressions of care, love, acceptance and positive attention. Control includes the setting of limits, establishment of rules and general exercise of parental authority. The various combinations of high and low levels of nurturance and control have been studied to determine how they contribute to (or detract from) the development of a healthy personality in children.

The major principle which runs throughout the various Schaeffer findings is simply this: that the parent can impose a high level of control if he also provides high levels of nurturance. Lots of love plus lots of discipline is a good combination, it seems. The negative side effects of too much authority occur only when that authority is not accompanied by an equivalently high level of nurturance.

That insight into natural parenting has obvious

implications for the church. If the standards of Christian living are to be taken seriously by a church, they must be taught in an atmosphere of loving, accepting spiritual nurture. When a church is accepting of an individual only to the extent that he or she meets their standards of behavior, that church misses the whole point of God's fatherliness, of his unrelenting, noncontingent love.

When is a youth leader, a pastor or a parent doing the job of rearing children with balance? When we do it in a fashion which most resembles the style of God himself. He was, and is, the ultimate parent and teacher.

13

AN APPEAL FOR SOFT FATHERS

■

Every father understands that it is his duty to put food on the table and clothing on the backs of his little children. To provide such basic material needs is universally agreed to be the irreducible minimum in a father's responsibility.

The best father, however, realizes that the job of providing for his children has just begun when the groceries are bought and the rent is paid. The best fathers also provide love, a special brand of masculine love only a father can give. For a father who is deeply involved in his role as provider and breadwinner, taking the time to make direct expressions of love and affection for his child can seem unnecessary or even awkward. "I work hard all day to provide for my family, and that is my expression of love," reasons the father. But that is not good enough. The father's responsibility does not end when he has put food on the table. A good father also shows his children love through direct expressions of affection.

Lee Salk, a well-known psychiatrist, has written a book titled *My Father, My Son*, in which he interviews scores of young men about their relationships with their fathers and draws some conclusions based on these interviews. One of the most interesting sections in this fascinating book is Salk's explanation of the need so many boys and men express for a more loving, caring father. Over and over the interviews describe respect and admiration for their fathers but also regret that there had not been more overt expressions of love between them. "Not one male interviewed," reports Salk, "wished his father had been *less* demonstrative. No one said, 'My father was demonstrative, but I won't be that way with my son.' "

Salk summarizes this commonly expressed desire for closer contact with our fathers by referring to his own experience: "Caring is one thing. I mean, my father cared more about us than anything in the world, but he cared from afar. What matters is to be there on a daily basis . . . . I believe the most important thing about a father is his love—expressed in a real sense. Not just saying, 'Hey, I love you,' and letting it go at that. The most important thing in our relationship were those talks we had . . . after I got to know him and we had shed a few tears and had dropped all our defenses and our retention of emotions, and could look eye to eye, man to man, and say, 'I love you.' "

I once asked my students at Lee College to describe for me the single best memory they had of their fathers. Whether the event occurred 10 years earlier or a year or a week, I instructed them to select the single slice of memory by which they most fondly remembered their father.

The responses were predictably varied, but probably the most common memories were those in which the child and father had shared a small moment— memories in which the dominant theme was simply being together, doing something of no particular importance, but doing it together. Here are some examples:

• "When he came home from work, pulled me into his arms, then put me on his shoulders. I felt so loved."

• "My dad taking the family camping, and he always tended to the fire made to keep warm in the evening. He always took charge when we were in the mountains."

• "The best memory I have had with my father was the day we played a game of chase in the back yard when I was about 7 years old."

• "My father and I used to go fishing a lot, and I would steer the boat while he fished. The type of fishing we did was done at dusk and on into the early night. He sat in the front of the boat with a 24-foot cane pole, which had bait on a hook hanging about 12 inches down, and he would slap the water with the end of the pole (jigger fishing). I remember those fishing trips."

My own answer to the same question—"What is your single most positive memory of your father?"—is consistent with the pattern seen in these students' memories. I have shared many good times with my father, not only when I was a youngster but in adulthood as well. I have lived near him and have worked professionally with him, until his retirement five years ago. I enjoy hundreds of pleasant memories of him as a father. But when asked to recall a single memory which stands out as the warmest and best, I find myself remembering a particular moment from more than 35 years ago.

I was a boy, not even a teenager. Two of my brothers and I had accompanied Dad on a trip to camp meeting someplace in the Deep South. We were returning to our home in Tennessee late one night, driving the roomy old Buick. It was past midnight. I remember the darkness, the headlights probing the black road ahead as we pushed through the night.

My brothers had fallen asleep on the backseat; I alone remained awake with Dad in the front. I remember feeling that he was pleased that I was still awake to keep him company, and the sense of his unspoken welcome made me feel important to him. We rarely spoke. Occasionally there was a comment from one to the other, but no great intimacies were shared, not even a casual conversation. We were just there together, sitting in the dark; and to me the feeling of privacy and warmth, being with Dad with no competition for his attention, in no hurry to move on to anything else, was a delicious sensation that still resonates in my memory after all these years.

With children, there is sometimes no substitute for parental time—periods of unhurried, undivided attention. Often even the best parents forget that need or develop lifestyles which provide no room for it. We find ourselves so problem-oriented as parents that we spend most of our time with our children as troubleshooters. When our child needs our help— whether to tie his shoes or to get a driver's license—we address the problem, help as best we can and move on. But often there is no particular thing our children need from us; what they need is just for us to be there.

A friend told me of a time when his daughter stepped quietly into his study as he worked at his desk. Looking up as the child entered, he asked her, "What can I do for you, sweetheart?"

"Nothing," she replied timidly, as though unprepared for the question. "I just want to be where you are."

He realized as she answered how much like a

client he had treated her. She appeared at his door, and he immediately thought of her in terms of something to be done, a small domestic problem to be solved, a "daughter-client" to be served. He moved instinctively to do for her when all she wanted was for him to be there.

Lee Salk observes, "One of the most malignant elements in the father-son relationship is proximity without communication." That the old man is always around, that he is always watching, can be an oppressive experience, rather than a supportive one if there is never any positive, loving conversation between the child and him. The presence of our father becomes a positive part of our lives only if we are interacting with him in a loving way. Otherwise, he is at best a piece of furniture, at worst a bothersome watchdog.

Some fathers have difficulty showing their children the warmth and love they feel. Their love is deep and genuine, but they are awkward in expressing it overtly and consequently don't try very often. Such fathers show their love by working hard and providing for the family rather than expressing it in more personal ways. Touching and kissing and saying "I love you" are not what real love is all about, they reason; supporting the needs of one's family is what a father's love is all about.

That is a common view of fatherhood; the problem with it is that it is only half right. The truth is that children need the touching and kissing and saying "I love you." They need it, in fact, maybe as much as they need shelter and a hot meal at night. The home that lacks continual expressions of warmth and personal affection is an impoverished home just as surely as if there were no bread on the table or no heat in the furnace.

For whatever cultural or biological reasons, mothers have a special touch, a special warmth that fathers often lack in communicating personal love for their children. Simple gestures of affection, stroking and touching, a sense of acceptance and concern—in short, all those qualities which add up to warm, nurturing parenthood—seem to come more easily to mothers than to fathers and, consequently, are left to mothers in millions of homes. Christopher Leach, a British writer and father, described the special communication between mother and child in a particularly poignant way: "Children come from within the mother. A man shares; but he cannot truly know."

So father wins the bread and provides the discipline while mother nurtures and encourages and kisses the scraped knees and bruised feelings of the child. With that separation of roles, the job gets done. At least that is the old-fashioned model. Fortunately for both the children and their fathers, this traditional model of the father as a "strong, silent type" is gradually losing ground. More young fathers are accepting their responsibility in the nurture of their children. More dads are learning how to be motherly, and this is a positive development for the entire family. When a man learns that it is not unmanly to show affection, that he is not being soft or feminine when he expresses love in overt and emotional ways, both he and his children are the better for it.

CHAPTER 14

COMMUNICATING WITH YOUNG PEOPLE

■

At the heart of good relationships with teenagers is healthy communication. Adults who can communicate effectively with their children are generally adults who can solve problems as they arise and whose values are most likely to be transmitted to the next generation.

An Atlanta sportswriter once wrote of Pepper Rodgers, the Georgia Tech football coach: "Pepper has a speech impediment; he doesn't know how to listen."

Many of us have that same kind of "speech impediment." We spend so much of our time talking *at* our children and *to* our children and *about* our children that we rarely take time to hear *from* our children.

Dr. Robert Fisher is an insightful psychologist as

well as a fine preacher. In his book *The Language of Love*, he tells an amusing story that shows the degree to which listening is a major part of the whole process of communication. While a college student, he was hitchhiking in California and was picked up by a solitary motorist: "As we began to journey together, he started talking and I started listening. To my surprise, as I paid close attention to what he was saying, I found myself genuinely interested and involved in the conversation. Occasionally I would make a comment or ask a pertinent question, but I was never asked and never gave any information about myself. The time passed quickly, and soon we were in Bakersfield. We came to the crossroads where he was to turn off. Instead, he decided to take me to another main intersection 10 miles or so further on where he thought my chances of getting a ride would be better. As we traveled on, he kept talking and I kept listening. When we arrived at our new destination, he remarked that he had never seen so few cars on the road. I might have a difficult time getting picked up there, he said, so he would take me to the base of the Ridge Route . . . that was another 15 miles. He kept talking; I kept listening.

"As we came to the Ridge Route, he had to make a decision. Was he going to take me over the mountain into Southern California (about 75 miles), or was he going to let me out, turn around and go back home? 'I can't believe this traffic,' he said. 'You know, I don't have anything important to do today.

I'm going to take you on over the mountain.' An hour or so later we arrived in San Fernando Valley.

"During all our time together he had never asked me anything about myself, not even my name. He had told me about his family, his business, his dreams and ambitions. I forgot about trying to impress him by telling him about myself. I found it interesting and stimulating to learn so much about another person. I thoroughly enjoyed the conversation . . . as I got out and was about to close the car door, he stopped me.

" 'Just a minute, young man, before you go I want to tell you something. I make a habit of picking up hitchhikers. I like to learn about other people. I enjoy a good conversation.' He paused and became more serious. 'I know you're young,' he said, 'but I want you to know you are absolutely one of the finest conversationalists I have ever met.' "

Many of our children would think we had suddenly become great conversationalists if we would stop talking and begin to listen to them for a change. We might be surprised at some of the things we would learn.

Dr. James Mallory is a born-again Presbyterian who is also a psychiatrist and medical director of the Atlanta Counseling Center. He and I have lectured together in various settings, and I have been struck by the practical help he offers parents and church workers who are trying to communicate more effectively with teenagers. Here are some of his tips on the subjects, gleaned from my notes and paraphrased broadly:

1.   Avoid "collective monologue."

This is a conversation in which the two parties are not really exchanging ideas at all but are merely engaged in two separate monologues. One makes a short speech, then waits for the other to make a short speech before it is his time again. This is not dialogue at all, and very little real communication is occurring. Good conversation is like a tennis match; when the person with whom you are playing hits the ball to you, you hit it back toward him. In collective monologue, this doesn't happen; instead, both players are throwing balls up into the air and hitting them past the other person.

2.   Seek to address the problem rather than ascribing blame.

In most cases the question of who is to blame for a problem is a nonconstructive one to begin with. Blame placing wastes time and creates negative feelings all the way around. It is far better to move immediately to the problem at hand: What do we do from here?

3.   Don't come on immediately with advice.

The adult who responds to a child's dilemma with pat answers is sending the message to the child that he doesn't regard the problem as being very difficult or complex. It implies that the problem is too simple. Even if you think you know the solution to the child's problem, it is a good idea to wait a while, listen while the child fully explores all aspects of the situation, then give advice if it is appropriate to do so. Often the child will talk his own way through to the same solution you would have given but will be far more ready to accept it.

4. Be confidential.

This is not only a good practice for professionals but for parents as well. Many well-intentioned parents discourage their children from confiding in them by spreading the information to friends, neighbors or other family members. One of the greatest inhibitors of good communication, especially for young people, is fear of being exposed or embarrassed. Children learn quickly whether we can be trusted to hold information in confidence, and having that trust can be valuable to family communication at every level.

5. Please touch.

Body language is important in all kinds of communication, and between parent and child it is particularly so. A touch, a pat on the shoulder, an embrace—all can be effective ways of breaking down the barriers of communication which sometimes develop between parents and their growing children. This is obviously easier with a teenager if a parent has been physically affectionate throughout

125

the child's life, but it is never too late to begin showing physical closeness when communicating with children. Touching signals closeness and intimacy, and many children need such expressions as thirsty plants need water.

6. Don't feel you must point out all the inconsistencies in a child's statement.

Children and teenagers are not fully developed yet in a cognitive and intellectual sense, and there commonly are huge holes in their logic, particularly when they are emotionally involved in what they are trying to communicate. Too many times adults feel called upon to point out every inconsistency in whatever the child is saying. If these lapses of logic are critical to the decision that is being made or the point under dispute, it may be necessary to address them. But if they are simple adolescent overstatements or reflect the immature and changing opinions of a child, it serves no good purpose to point them out. It merely makes the parent some sort of "logic cop." This may satisfy the parent's sense of order, but it discourages open communication from the child.

7. Don't finish your child's sentences.

In any conversation it is offensive to interrupt someone who is talking, to finish sentences for them. Adults are particularly prone to do this when talking to children and teenagers. A parent or youth worker must avoid this temptation for two reasons:

(1) because teenagers are so unpredictable and you will frequently miss the point by barging ahead and (2) because they are more easily intimidated into silence and are prone to quit talking altogether if constantly preempted by an adult who rushes them along by anticipating what they will say next. It is important to give a child verbal feedback, letting him know you are listening, but your feedback should not "lead" him.

8. Don't play the role of district attorney.

This means that adults should stifle the urge to dig for details beyond those which are volunteered by the child. Communication between parents and their children often becomes a verbal tug-of-war, with the parent trying to pull from the child more information than he wishes to disclose. If this occurs frequently, the result is that the teenager stops sharing entirely. If whenever a child tells you A, you insist on knowing B and C, the child will soon learn to not bring up the subject at all. Here is the most familiar of all parent-child exchanges: "Where did you go?" "Out." "What did you do?" "Nothing." Does that bit of dialogue sound familiar? It is the common case of the parent digging for details the child doesn't want to give. When the adult responds instead with an interested but nonprosecutorial fashion, he may be amazed at how much information is ultimately volunteered.

9. Encourage the child to enlarge on what he says.

This is different from digging for more details, for here the adult is not seeking more information beyond what is offered, but rather asks questions which encourage the child to elaborate on his feelings and opinions about things he has already said. "Why do you feel that way?" "It sounds as if you feel strongly about this." These are the types of statements and questions which elicit from the child additional expressions without seeming to push for more disclosure than that with which he feels comfortable.

10. Don't resort to euphemisms.

In communication with children, it is especially important to say what one means rather than cloaking every utterance in allusion and innuendo. A child is not as adept at subtlety and reading between the lines as adults are, and it is common for parents to leave a conversation feeling they have said *one* thing while the child has heard something entirely different. Talking with children or teenagers is no time for veiled references and vague ideas. Be explicit; make sure the child understands the words and concepts you are using. Don't assume he automatically understands the metaphors and socially accepted code words we adults find familiar.

15

THE PARENT
AS MODEL

■

Clearly the most critical function parents serve in the lives of their children is that of *modeling*. They are many things for their children—providers, teachers, givers of emotional support, disciplinarians, chauffeurs, homework tutors, cheerleaders and night watchmen—but most of all they are models.

Modeling is the most powerful type of learning. It is a far more basic psychological process than other types of learning because it occurs at both the conscious and the unconscious level. It takes place whether the parent or child is aware of it or not. When our children do things the way we do them in a more-or-less deliberate attempt to learn, that is simple imitative learning; when they find themselves unconsciously becoming *like* us in a thousand small ways, that is pure modeling.

One of the most sobering aspects of modeling is

that it occurs even when we don't want it to occur; children model our undesirable traits as faithfully as our positive ones. Have you ever used that time-worn phrase, "Don't do as I do; do as I say"? That may be the most futile bit of wishful thinking in the parental vocabulary. To an impressive degree, all that we say is much less important than what we *are* in the presence of our children.

The power of this principle is beautifully expressed in a very familiar poem by Dorothy Law Nolte.

Children Learn What They Live

If a child lives with criticism,
   he learns to condemn.
If a child lives with hostility,
   he learns to fight.
If a child lives with fear,
   he learns to be apprehensive.
If a child lives with pity,
   he learns to feel sorry for himself.
If a child lives with ridicule,
   he learns to be shy.
If a child lives with jealousy,
   he learns what envy is.
If a child lives with shame,
   he learns to feel guilty.
If a child lives with encouragement,
   he learns to be confident.
If a child lives with tolerance,
   he learns to be patient.
If a child lives with praise,
   he learns to be appreciative.

If a child lives with acceptance,
    he learns to love.
If a child lives with approval,
    he learns to like himself.
If a child lives with recognition,
    he learns it is good to have a goal.
If a child lives with sharing,
    he learns about generosity.
If a child lives with honesty and fairness,
    he learns what truth and justice are.
If a child lives with security,
    he learns to have faith in himself and
    in those about him.
If a child lives with friendliness,
    he learns that the world is a nice place
    in which to live.
If you live with serenity,
    your child will live with peace of mind.

When our words do not match our behavior, it is almost always the behavior, not the words, that will be the child's teacher.

This emphasis on modeling can be rather daunting to typical Christian parents or youth workers who are sharply aware of their own imperfections, and for good reason. Sometimes we are more adept at fooling ourselves than we are at fooling our children. When our children grow into adolescence and their own behavior patterns and attitudes toward God and the church begin to emerge, it can be almost like holding up to ourselves a mirror that lets us see ourselves as we really are. We see the true, unvarnished image of ourselves reflected in the way our children model after us, and that can and should drive us to our knees at times.

On the other hand, this powerful force of modeling can also be a wonderful blessing to parents for the very same reason that it operates at such a deep level of honesty. There is a large amount of hope in that. There is the assurance that many of the most deeply held values which we are unable to explain adequately to our children will be communicated and imparted to them through modeling. Some of the spiritual principles we embrace most profoundly are those which are difficult to "teach" in a conscious and logical way. But they can be shared with our young people even when we cannot fully articulate them ourselves.

The late Lawrence Kohlberg, who studied the way children develop a sense of what is right and wrong, was fond of saying, "Values are caught, not taught." By that he meant they are so pervasive in a particular social atmosphere they are virtually contagious. Figuratively speaking, they are breathed in and absorbed from the environment of which the children are a part.

The need for parents and youth workers who model a spiritual value system and mind-set is made even more urgent by the deepening swamp of evil our contemporary culture has become. The messages that flood our young people, in both overt and subtle ways, all conspire to push them away from God or even a lifestyle of simple decency and self-discipline.

Consider the hypocrisy of television advertising that ignores the human wreckage caused by alcohol while relentlessly pitching to teenagers the message that drinking is not only a necessary ingredient of the "good life," it is central to it. The major breweries do not merely advertise their wares; they engage in a constant campaign to show drinking as a natural pastime of the entire college-age population. Meanwhile, they strike the rather pious posture of being concerned about excessive drinking with occasional "Know when to say no" ads.

The evidence shows, however, that the concern with the damage of excessive drinking in our society is not balanced to any degree with the message that drinking is the thing to do. The major breweries now spend $847 million a year on beer advertising alone on television—an amount that has doubled since 1980! Most of the extra dollars have gone into ads specifically aimed at the teen and college-age market.

A recent report in the Boston *Globe*, which can hardly be considered a conservative publication, offers this analysis: "Behind the frothy beer-industry ads featuring 'babes' in bikinis, the crooning of pop idols, and the awkward buffoonery of comedian Joe Piscopo rages a hard-fought battle over a big target: the American teenager." It is clear that the liquor industry in America is not seeking to sell its product primarily to mature, thinking adults but to teenagers whose values are still being formed. It should be no surprise that their major sales technique is the subtle communication that almost amounts to media brainwashing.

The *Globe* reports that "the beer industry has gone beyond mere advertising and promotion to enter successfully nearly every facet of public life in America in the last decade. Although the industry denies specifically targeting teenagers, critics say much of its advertising—replete with the language, fashions and idols of teenagers—promotes underage drinking. Two recent commercials, featuring animated graphics, sexual innuendoes and jokes about beer ads, 'will attract teenagers like Clearasil to a nose pimple,' wrote Bob Garfield, a columnist for *Advertising Age*, an advertising industry publication."

It is inevitable that as such concentrated media firepower to sell teenagers on alcohol has increased, the consumption—and related problems—has increased correspondingly. Consider these alarming facts: Fifty-six percent of high school students in America begin drinking beer in ninth grade or earlier. Eighteen percent of all drivers in fatal auto accidents last year were teenagers. The number one cause of death among teenagers—accounting for 40 percent—is auto accidents. In 1988 nearly 24,000 people died in alcohol-related accidents, with over half a million others injured.

At least one individual the alcohol industry has used as a role model to sell beer to young people has quit as a result of his concern that the youth culture is increasingly being made into a culture of drinking. The *Globe* reports: "Bubba Smith, the former professional football player, dropped his role in Lite Beer commercials after serving as grand marshal in a homecoming parade at his alma mater, Michigan State University. 'I thought everyone was very fired up,' Smith said at the time. 'All of a sudden, one side of the street started saying, "Tastes great," and the other side would answer, "Less filling." It just totally freaked me out. When I went to the bonfire, they were just completely drunk out of their heads.' "

The pattern is clear: First, football is used to sell drinking; soon the drinking becomes more important than the football. An executive in the movie industry recently observed that theaters have become "places to sell popcorn." To a large degree, the beer industry is succeeding in making sports events, concerts and such traditions as spring break little more than excuses to sell beer.

A former director of the Division of Alcoholism in New York put it this way: "Advertising doesn't create cultural trends; it capitalizes on them. The brewers didn't dream up spring break, but because of the amount of money invested in it, they can shape what comes out. The underlying message is that it is naturally a part of college life to drink, and that is potentially the most damaging to youngsters."

It is this deluge of secular and self-destructive images which makes the need for positive parental modeling more critical in this generation than ever before. If ever there was a time for "hands-on" parenting, it is the 1990s. Parents who do not give high priority to the time personally spent with their children, exposing them to positive modeling and values, are leaving a vacuum into which the hedonistic mind-set of this age will flow.

A parent's responsibility to model personally the values of Christ cannot be delegated. It is a task that cannot be done by pastors or youth ministers, no matter how committed or godly.

Dr. Robert Coles is one of the nation's most respected analysts of the development of children and adolescents in our society. He recently wrote: "I think what children in the United States desperately need is a moral purpose, and a lot of our children here aren't getting that. They're getting parents who are very concerned about getting them into the right colleges, buying the best clothing for them, giving them an opportunity to live in neighborhoods where they'll lead fine and affluent lives and where they can be given the best toys, go on interesting vaca-

THE PARENT AS MODEL

tions, and all sorts of things.

"Parents work very hard these days; and they're acquiring things that they feel are important for their children. And yet vastly more important are things that are not happening. They're not spending time with their children, at least not very much."

If this warning is appropriate for even secular parents, how much more should it challenge Christians, who are transmitting not only cultural values but spiritual ones as well! In parenting, there is no substitute for time; and there is no time like personal, one-on-one time in which the parent *shows* the child how to live, think, react and serve God in a secular age.

CHAPTER
16

STRIKING A BALANCE

■

In our effort to bring up children for the kingdom of God, we find ourselves seeking to strike a balance between two sets of equally desirable values. As in so much of life, the key to good Christian discipling seems to be our ability to find the middle ground between opposite and competing demands.

Striking such a balance requires the best effort of both parents and youth leaders. Consider how many situations exist in which the importance of competing values must be weighed against one another in the process of working with teenagers in the church:

• We must provide specialized and youth-oriented programming for them within the church . . . and yet we must integrate youth into the worship and life of the church body as a whole.

• We must allow their church activities to be entertaining and attractive ... and yet we must guarantee that they are fed the meat of God's Word and given truly spiritual training rather than simply being ecclesiastical baby-sitters.

• We must understand that as adolescents they have a growing desire for freedom from adult supervision ... and yet we must provide for them enough rules and limits that they know what the laws of God and nature require of them in the real world.

• We must show them that the church cares for them and is there for them in their times of need ... and yet we must teach them that the church is not primarily a place to be served but a place to be of service to God and others.

• We must teach them that the family of God is a large and diverse family, that there are many different ways of expressing biblical discipleship other than those of our own tradition ... and yet we must instill in them a deep pride in the Church of God, a love for our denomination and its history and traditions, and a positive understanding of what that means in the larger context of the Kingdom.

• We must transmit to them a respect for the authority God places in the church and the need to submit to that authority ... and yet teach them how, when principle is at stake, to disagree agreeably— how to be part of a "loyal opposition" when they are in the minority.

• We must recognize that adolescence is a unique period in the human developmental sequence and that teenagers have their own special characteristics . . . and yet we must keep in mind that they are human just like everyone else and that in many respects they have the same feelings and needs we had at that age.

• We must attempt to give them special teaching in the specific topics that are part of the modern world in which they live . . . and yet we must continue to teach them the ageless stories and concepts found in Scripture, which are no less relevant now than ever.

• We must keep them busy with a wide variety of activities and programs, understanding that they have the attention span of a strobe light and are easily bored . . . and yet we must not so overprogram their lives that there is never time to get to know them, to let them think, to show them how to be still and hear from God.

• As ministers or parents we must maintain a level of personal and spiritual authority which will form a basis for the discipline and leadership we must impose . . . and yet we must be personal and "real" enough to allow true intimacy to develop between us and them on the personal basis of friend to friend.

• We must be willing to reveal our feet of clay enough to show that we are also human . . . and yet we must be role models of purity and strength, offering them a standard worthy of their aspirations.

• We must allow them their own space, permit them room to be individuals and to express their individuality, not expecting them to do and be exactly like everyone else in the family or the youth group . . . if you can and yet we must not allow them to become detached loners but must teach them how important it is to be a part of the team, the family, the body of Christ, that sometimes one must give up a bit of his legitimate individuality in order to participate in the life of the larger whole.

• We must encourage them to reach for success in all their pursuits, to be the best scholars, athletes, young businessmen they can possibly be . . . and yet we must warn them that spiritual priorities are higher than natural ones and that sometimes we give up a chance to be number one in the world's eyes in order to follow God's will for us.

• We must shelter and protect them from the horrible sinfulness of a debauched society . . . and yet allow them enough exposure to this culture that they gradually develop their own spiritual muscle and personal faith.

• We must be the source of high expectations for them, knowing they will usually live up to whatever expectations we communicate and rise to the level we set . . . and yet we must be the source of noncontingent acceptance and love, which demonstrates that we love them regardless of what they do or achieve.

• We must be open to dialogue and contrary opinions, understanding that often their challenges to our views are merely a way of testing our openness . . . and yet we must be firm advocates of a specific viewpoint, giving them the intellectual anchor they need.

• We must see them as essentially spiritual beings, all of whose crises of change are in some way related to their spiritual nature . . . and yet we must be careful not to overanalyze every move they make, constantly taking their pulse, "spiritualizing" even the most normal developmental events.

Matching up to the challenge of such a list is enough to buckle the knees of the most confident parent or youth leader among us.

Our only hope of meeting the challenge lies in the enabling power of the Holy Spirit. Every parent, every minister who loves his young people, every lay youth leader—all of us must remember that the battle is the Lord's. We can only do our best and leave the rest with Him.

In the words of a very old axiom, we work as if everything depends on us, and we pray as if everything depends on God. Then we trust in His power to achieve the final results. They are, after all, His children too.

WRITTEN REVIEW

Dad, Mom and the Church: Raising Children Together / CTC 708

Instructions

1. A Certificate of Credit will be awarded when the student satisfies the requirements listed on page 6.
2. The student, at a time designated by the instructor, should search the text for the answers to the review questions. These should be written on a blank sheet of paper and presented to the instructor for processing.
3. In the case of home study, the student should present his answers to the pastor or to someone the pastor designates.

Questions

1. True or false. It is harder to bring up a young man or woman to love and serve Christ than it has ever been before.
2. Complete this sentence: "The evils have always been present, but never like today, _____."
3. What is the *critical task* in bringing up children for God?
4. What is meant by the terms *upside* and *downside* of sin or faith?
5. Name the four foundations of discipling youth.
6. Where do all heartfelt experiences originate?
7. What is the deadliest spiritual habit into which teenagers fall?
8. Why do we engage in the service of God?
9. What is the key role played by each of the following members of the triangular relationship heading our youth ministry?   a. The senior pastor b. Youth leader c. Parents
10. Fill in the missing words: "The goal of the church is not to give kids a _____ but to give them the gospel. It is spiritual values, not _____, which the church seeks to impart."
11. Explain the "solar system" approach to youth ministry.
12. What is the best explanation you can give your child as to why your family is committed to regular church attendance?
13. How does a parent gain credibility with children, especially as they grow older?
14. Fill in the missing words: "The church must serve the function of both _____ and _____ in the world; it must attack _____ with prophetic zeal while befriending the _____ with priestly tenderness."
15. What do the "best" fathers provide besides groceries, rent and so on?
16. What is it that we rarely take time to do because we spend so much time talking *at* our children and *to* our children and *about* our children?
17. When our words do not match our behavior, which will most often be the child's teacher?
18. Complete this sentence: "In parenting there is no substitute for time, and there is no time like personal, one-on-one time in which the parent *shows* the child _____."
19. What does the author mean by "we find ourselves seeking to strike a balance between two sets of equally desirable values"?
20. What is our only hope for meeting the challenge of raising spiritually fit children?